A note to teachers and parents...

The Essentials of Key Stage 2 English is fully aligned to the National Curriculum Key Stage 2 English framework.

The book has been produced to meet with specific criteria:

- To produce excellent revision notes for the end of Key Stage 2 National Curriculum Tests (SATs) for levels 3–5 inclusive.
- To encourage and retain the interest of pupils at Key Stage 2.
- To cover the material without reference to specific levels. All pupils should be encouraged to cover as much as possible of every topic.
- To help teachers and parents by providing a concise summary of the work that is covered throughout school years 3–6.

Practice is provided in the accompanying Pupil Worksheets, which incorporate questions and activities to help pupils prepare for the tests and practise their skills.

A note about the author...

Christine Moorcroft taught in primary and special schools before moving into an advisory post, followed by lecturing and Ofsted inspection. She has also worked for an educational publishing company and is now a full-time writer of text books, guides and workbooks for children aged 4–14 and their teachers and parents. Her work includes more than a hundred books on different aspects of teaching and learning English.

A note to pupils...

We're sure you will enjoy using this book, but here are some tips to help you to get the most out of it:

- Read each section carefully and test yourself as you go along.
- Try to get into a routine. Work through the book steadily. Don't try to do too much at once.

This table shows the structure of the Key Stage 2 English National Curriculum Tests (SATs) which you will normally sit in Year 6, at the end of Key Stage 2.

	Test	Time Allowed	Marks
Reading	Reading Task	1 hour (15 mins reading time, 45 mins answering time)	50
Writing	Longer Task (including handwriting*)	45 mins	31
	Shorter Task	20 mins	12
	Spelling Test	10 minutes	7
Total			100

*Handwriting is also assessed in this test. Handwriting should be clear, fluent and consistent.

In the reading test you will be given a booklet containing a selection of non-fiction pieces and a separate question and answer booklet.

The longer writing test will ask you to plan and write a story or a non-fiction text. You will be given a booklet with instructions and space for planning, and a separate answer booklet.

The shorter writing test will ask you to write a story or a non-fiction text. You will be given an instruction booklet with limited space to write your answer. The booklet will also contain the spelling test which your teacher will go through with you.

Contents

Punctuation, Grammar and Spelling

Reading

Contents

Writing

Writing Fiction

Writing Non-Fiction

Punctuation

Punctuation

It is very important to use punctuation correctly in your writing so that what you write means the same to your reader as it does to you. There are a number of punctuation marks which you need to learn how to use correctly.

Full Stop

A full stop marks the end of a sentence:
– The swans swam in a circle.

It is also used after abbreviated words:
– Ave. (Avenue), approx. (approximately).

Comma

A comma can be used in three ways:

1 To separate items in a list:
– Sam had a walnut, some string, two marbles and a toffee.

2 To make the meaning clear:
– Jess saw a dog, and a woman carrying a baby.

Without a comma, this sentence could mean that Jess saw a dog helping a woman to carry a baby! With the comma, there is no confusion; the sentence means that Jess saw a woman carrying a baby, and she saw a dog.

3 To surround extra information added to a sentence (see parentheses on page 6).

Question Mark

A question mark is used at the end of a sentence which asks a question:
– What time is it?
– May I go out tonight?

Exclamation Mark

An exclamation mark is used to communicate feelings such as surprise, shock or horror. It can also show that something is urgent or funny.

The exclamation mark can come at the end of a sentence or it can follow a single word:
– My cat eats cereal for breakfast – mice crispies!
– Yuck!

It can be used after a command such as 'Go!'

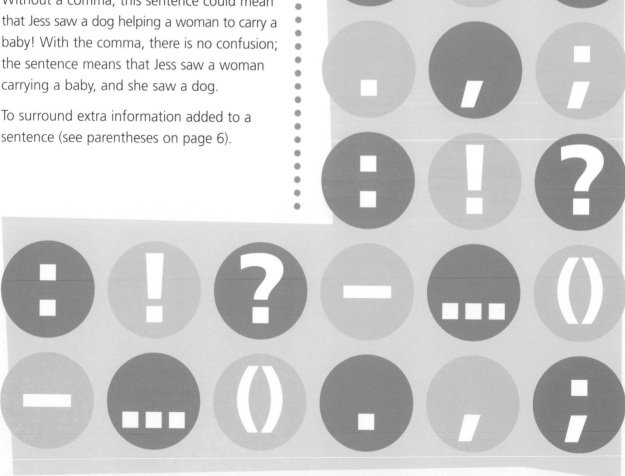

Apostrophe

An apostrophe is used in two ways:

1 To show contractions, i.e. to show that letters have been missed out:
- it's = it is
- don't = do not
- you're = you are

2 To show ownership:
- Jake's car.

After a singular noun (e.g. the girl) the apostrophe comes **before** the 's':
- the girl's bike (the bike belonging to the girl)
- Tom's jacket (the jacket belonging to Tom).

After a plural noun (e.g. the girls) the apostrophe comes **after** the 's':
- the girls' bike (the bike belonging to the girls)
- the Smiths' house (the house belonging to the Smiths)
- the ladies' cloakroom (the cloakroom belonging to the ladies).

If a plural noun does not end in 's' (e.g. men), the apostrophe comes **before** the 's':
- the men's toilets (the toilets belonging to the men)
- the children's home (the home belonging to the children).

> Never use an apostrophe when you make a word plural:
> - the cat's slept   ✗
> - the cats slept   ✔

> Never use an apostrophe in pronouns like hers, theirs, its, yours.
>
> Remember, **it's = it is**
> - it's a long way back
> **Its = belonging to it**
> - the dog ate its food

Colon

A colon can be used before an explanation:
- Ella learned something new: how to wire a plug.

It can also be used before an example or list:
- We saw three cars: a Volvo, a BMW and a Honda.

The part before the colon must make sense as a sentence but the part after it does not need to.

Semicolon

Semicolons can be used between closely related clauses instead of writing separate sentences:
- Like Charlotte, Jane was a good dancer; unlike her, she could not sing.

The parts before and after the semicolon can usually make sense as separate sentences.

Semicolons are also used to separate long items in a list. The list could be introduced with a colon:
- There were three raffle prizes: a week's holiday for two at a four-star hotel; a four-course dinner for two at the Café Royal; and a deluxe food hamper.

Punctuation

Parentheses

Parentheses are commas, brackets or dashes which are used to surround part of a sentence. This part of the sentence gives extra information or an explanation, but it does not need to be there for the rest of the sentence to make sense.

The coloured parts in the sentences below could be taken out and the sentences would still make sense.

- **Commas**
  - Salim, who wanted to win the race, had trained every day for months.
  - Tom, the football captain, scored two goals.

- **Brackets**
  Brackets are usually used when an explanation is being added:
  - Elvira Martinez (the star of the film) swept along the red carpet wearing a stunning silk gown.
  - He said that there was a poltergeist (mischievous ghost) in the house.

- **Dashes**
  Dashes are usually used when adding detail:
  - From his bedroom window – at the front of the house – he could see the mountains.
  - The boys were playing – very irresponsibly – in the road.

  A dash can also be used to separate one part of a sentence from the other:
  - I'm going to pick some flowers – lots of them.

Speech Marks (Quotation Marks)

Speech marks surround words which are spoken. Single quotes (' ') or double quotes (" ") can be used.
- 'I think it might rain, so I'll bring an umbrella,' said Nina.

When a spoken sentence is split into two parts by the speaker's name and 'said' (or another word for 'said'), the spoken words in the second part do not need a capital letter:
- 'I think it might rain,' said Nina, 'so I'll bring an umbrella.'

Only use a capital letter if it is a new sentence:
- 'I think it might rain so I'll bring an umbrella', said Nina. 'We don't want to ruin our hair!'

> Only the spoken words should be between speech marks.
>
> If the spoken words follow 'said' (or another word for 'said') there should be a comma between 'said' and the first speech mark, e.g.
> - Mum said, 'Let's see.'
>
> Punctuation marks (e.g. full stops, question marks) at the end of the spoken words come before the second speech mark, e.g.
> - 'Let's go!'

Clarity and Ambiguity

Clarity means being clear. Ambiguity means having more than one possible meaning.

The reader may interpret a sentence to mean something different from what the writer intended.

Punctuation makes your meaning clear. This is why it is important to use punctuation in your writing and why it is so important to use it correctly.

You can change the meaning of some sentences by changing only the punctuation:

- 'I don't know Sarah,' said Anhil.
  (Anhil does not know who Sarah is.)
- 'I don't know, Sarah,' said Anhil.
  (Anhil doesn't know the answer to Sarah's question.)

- 'Is this coat yours?' Amy asked Jake.
  (Amy asks Jake if the coat belongs to him.)
- 'Is this coat yours, Amy?' asked Jake.
  (Jake asks Amy if the coat belongs to her.)

Look at the following notices. The lack of punctuation makes their meanings ambiguous.

ELEPHANTS PLEASE STAY IN YOUR CAR

MAN EATING SHARK

SLOW HEDGEHOGS CROSSING

When punctuation is added, their meanings become clear (see opposite).

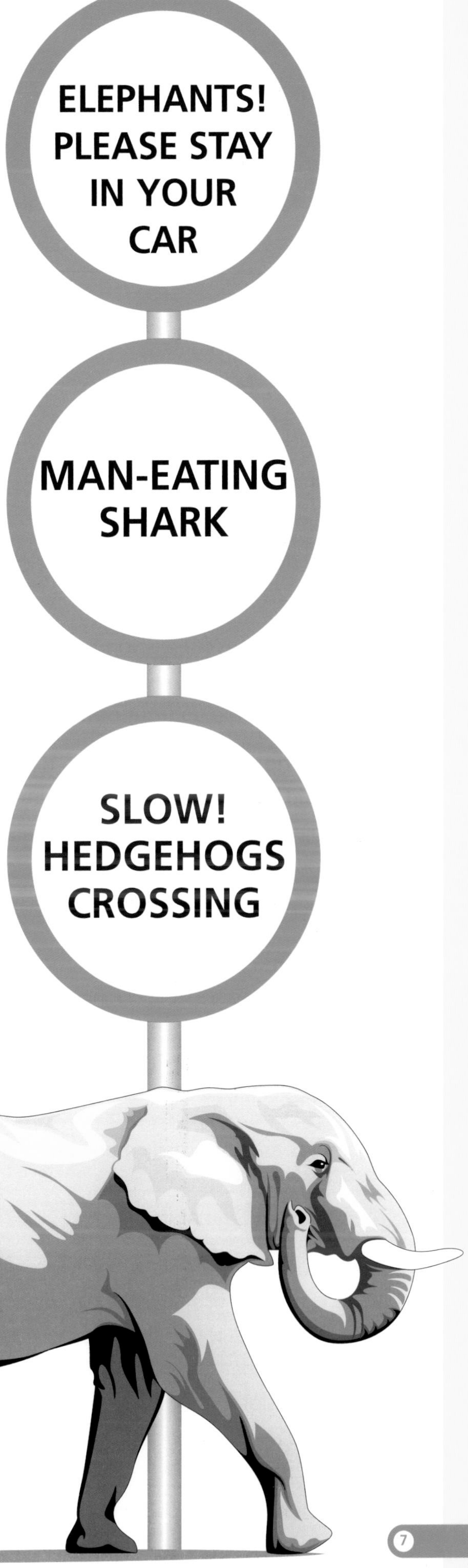

ELEPHANTS!
PLEASE STAY
IN YOUR
CAR

MAN-EATING
SHARK

SLOW!
HEDGEHOGS
CROSSING

Grammar

cloud

hill

lorry

car

bike

Word Classes

We group words into different classes, depending on the job they do in a sentence. The main word classes are nouns, pronouns, adjectives, verbs, adverbs and connectives.

Nouns

A **common noun** is a naming word, for example…
– lorry, car, bike, cloud, hill.

These are the names for any lorry, car, bike, cloud or hill. Common nouns can all be made plural and make sense with 'the' in front of them.

An **abstract noun** is a word used to name things like ideas and subjects. They are not actual physical objects, for example…
– geography, happiness, idea, luck, music.

Not all abstract nouns can be made plural.

A **proper noun** is the name of a particular person, place, pet, day, newspaper, organisation, etc. Proper nouns begin with a capital letter, for example…
– Adam, London, Rex, Saturday, *Daily Telegraph*, Marks and Spencer.

Proper nouns are not usually made plural but plurals are possible, for example…
– There are two Emmas in the class.

A **compound noun** is a noun made up of two words. The two words may be joined by a hyphen or may be joined to form one word, for example…
– clothes-peg, coat-hanger, traffic-light, night-light, slot-machine.
– airport, bookshop, dishcloth, hillside, outcome, riverbank, runway, staircase.

Pronouns

Pronouns can be used instead of nouns so that the noun is not repeated too often. Pronouns are words like 'this', 'that', 'those', 'who', 'which'.

Personal pronouns refer to people and objects so they can be used instead of common nouns and proper nouns. The personal pronouns are listed in this table:

Person	Singular Personal Pronoun	Plural Personal Pronoun
first	I, me	we, us
second	you	you
third	he, she, it, him, her	they, them

You must make it clear which noun the pronoun stands for. Look at this example:
– **Ella** was walking along when **Ella** met **Andy**. **Andy** gave **Ella** an envelope. **Ella** opened **the envelope**.

The short passage above contains several proper nouns so it sounds repetitive. Read this example:
– **She** was walking along when **she** met **him**. **He** gave **her it**. **She** opened **it**.

All the nouns have been replaced by pronouns. But the passage is difficult to understand now, because we don't know who or what 'she', 'him' and 'it' are. Read this example:
– **Ella** was walking along when **she** met **Andy**. **He** gave **her an envelope**. **She** opened **it**.

This is better. The nouns are not repeated and we know who and what the pronouns stand for.

Possessive pronouns show ownership (belonging). They are used in place of a noun which would have an apostrophe.

Possessive pronouns never have an apostrophe.

– Jason's = **his**
– Rebecca's = **her** or **hers**
– the dog's = **its**
– the family's = **their** or **theirs**

The possessive pronouns are listed in this table:

Person	Singular Possessive Pronoun	Plural Possessive Pronoun
first second third	my, mine your, yours his, her, hers, its	our, ours your, yours their, theirs

– The bag is **mine**.
– **Your** hair looks nice.
– Jason took **his** dog for a walk.

Using Pronouns

You can make the meaning of a text clear by using pronouns carefully and in the correct places. The example below shows how pronouns can cause ambiguity and how the meaning can be made clear.

Ambiguous	Clear
If your baby does not like raw apple, stew it gently for a few minutes.	If your baby does not like it raw, stew the apple gently for a few minutes.

Common Mistakes with Pronouns

1
– She said, 'Come and stay with my brother and me'. ✔
– She said, 'Come and stay with my brother and I'. ✘

It is wrong to say, 'Come and stay with I' so it is also wrong to say, 'Come and stay with my brother and I'.

2
– She said, 'My brother and I went out'. ✔
– She said, 'My brother and me went out'. ✘

It is wrong to say, 'Me went out', so it is also wrong to say, 'My brother and me went out'.

Grammar

Adjectives

An adjective is a describing word. It describes a **noun**, for example…
- a **long** road
- a **green** plant
- **neat** writing.

Adjectives can help to communicate an image or idea to your reader. Adjectives with similar meanings can create different effects, for example…
- thin, slim, skinny, slender.

A 'skinny girl' does not have the same meaning as a 'slender girl'.

Other examples of adjectives with similar meanings include…
- old, antique, ancient, elderly
- red, crimson, scarlet, rosy
- big, huge, enormous
- sleepy, tired, exhausted.

Adjectives can make a big difference to a piece of writing. Try to choose interesting adjectives instead of ones which are used every day. Which of the following descriptive sentences do you think is the most effective?
- We had some nice bread.
- We had some warm, freshly baked bread.

Try putting two or three adjectives together, for example, 'The slender young girl.' But do not do this too often, or your work will become difficult to read.

Using a **thesaurus** can help you to find effective adjectives.

Comparatives and Superlatives

An adjective can become a **comparative**, usually by adding -er to the end. A comparative is used to describe something by comparing it with something else, e.g. big ⟶ bigg**er**.

An adjective can be changed to a **superlative**, usually by adding -est to the end. A superlative is used to describe something to the highest or lowest degree, e.g. big ⟶ bigg**est**.

The table below shows how adjectives can become comparatives and superlatives. Note that the endings of some adjectives change when -er and -est are added. Some comparatives and superlatives are completely different words.

Adjective	Comparative	Superlative
small	smaller	smallest
cold	colder	coldest
funny	funnier	funniest
good	better	best
bad	worse	worst
many	more	most

For longer adjectives, the comparative and superlative are formed by adding an extra word: more and most.

Adjective	Comparative	Superlative
delicious	more delicious	most delicious
beautiful	more beautiful	most beautiful

warm, freshly baked bread

Verbs

A verb is a 'doing' word, for example, ask, cry, look, sing, take, make, have. All sentences contain a verb:

- They **climbed** to the top of Snowdon.
- Paris **is** the capital city of France.
- We **like** broccoli.

Your choice of verb can help to communicate an image or idea to readers. The balloons opposite show three basic verbs plus a list of verbs with similar meanings to show how you can create different effects.

Tense

The tense of a verb tells us whether it is happening now (present), has already happened (past) or is going to happen (future), for example…

- **Present:** I am looking for my dog.
- **Past:** I looked for my dog.
- **Future:** I shall look for my dog.

To form different tenses, an ending (suffix) can be added and/or an auxiliary verb can be added. The auxiliary verbs are do, be, have, can, could, will, shall, would, should, may, might, must and ought.

Present	Past	Future
he walk**s**	he walk**ed**	he **will** walk
he **is** walk**ing**	he **was** walk**ing**	he **is going to** walk
he laugh**s**	he laugh**ed**	he **will** laugh
he is laugh**ing**	he **was** laugh**ing**	he **is going to** laugh

Sometimes, the past tense is formed by changing the spelling of the verb altogether:

Present	Past
he runs	he **ran**
he goes	he **went**
he eats	he **ate**
he thinks	he **thought**
he writes	he **wrote**
he wins	he **won**
he catches	he **caught**

Verbs meaning 'walk'
amble, creep, hobble, limp, march, plod, saunter, stagger

Verbs meaning 'say'
announce, declare, drawl, exclaim, mumble, mutter, shout, whisper

Verbs meaning 'eat'
chew, chomp, devour, gnaw, gobble, gulp, munch, nibble

Grammar

Active and Passive Voice

The following sentence has an active verb. It is in the active voice:

– The cat **scratched** the door.

The following sentence has a passive verb. It is in the passive voice:

– The door **was scratched by** the cat.

When a verb is active it is clear who or what does the action. When a verb is passive it is not always clear who or what does the action. For example, in the passive sentence above, we do not need to say 'by the cat':

– The door **was scratched**.

The table below shows how sentences can be active or passive. Some sentences read better in the active voice; others read better in the passive voice. Try to decide which sentence is better in the passive voice.

Active	Passive
The teacher will mark the tests.	The tests will be marked by the teacher.
The trees sheltered the plants.	The plants were sheltered by the trees.
Someone will serve dinner at 8 o'clock.	Dinner will be served at 8 o'clock.

Adverbs

An adverb is a describing word. It describes a **verb**, for example…

– He sang **loudly.**
– They jumped **high.**

- **Adverbs of manner** describe *how* an action is carried out:

The snake slithered.

How did it slither?

The snake slithered slowly.

Other adverbs of manner: carefully, happily, neatly, noisily, quickly, quietly, slowly.

- **Adverbs of place** describe *where* the action is carried out:

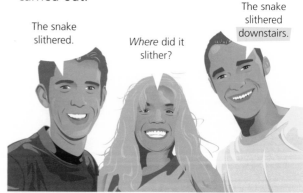

The snake slithered.

Where did it slither?

The snake slithered downstairs.

Other adverbs of place: anywhere, away, here, indoors, nowhere, outdoors, there, upstairs.

- **Adverbs of time** describe *when* the action is carried out:

The snake slithered.

When did the snake slither?

The snake slithered yesterday.

Other adverbs of time: today, tomorrow, earlier, later.

Connectives

Connectives link words, parts of sentences, paragraphs and sometimes even chapters. They tell us how events or facts relate to each other.

Conjunctions are simple connectives which join words, or groups of words, of equal importance, for example…
- She eats all kinds of vegetables <u>and</u> most types of fish.
- She eats all kinds of fish <u>but</u> never meat.

Prepositions are connectives which join words, or groups of words, to show a relationship between them:

Simple Relationships
- I know an old lady <u>who</u> swallowed a fly.
- This is the house <u>that</u> Jack is building.
- In the mist I could see two dark outlines <u>which</u> looked like houses.

Time Relationships
Time connectives show how words are related by time. They include the following: after, at the same time, before, in the meantime, next, later:
- I washed my hands <u>before</u> eating dinner.

Time connectives are very useful when writing stories.

Place Relationships
Place connectives show how words are related by place. They include the following: at, beside, under, up, above, below, next to:
- The cat was asleep <u>under</u> the dressing table.

Place connectives are useful when writing stories, explanations and instructions.

Logical Relationships
Logical connectives show how words are related by cause, reason or purpose. They include the following: due to, because, in order to, so, as a result:
- He bought plenty of food <u>so</u> we could have a barbecue.

Logical connectives are useful when writing explanations, discussions and persuasive texts.

PLANNING NOTICE

This is the house that Jack is building.

It is next to the river.

It will be finished before the end of the year.

Grammar

Sentences and Clauses

A clause is a group of words which contains a verb. A sentence is made up of one or more clauses.

Simple Sentences

Simple sentences contain only one clause. Therefore, they only contain one verb:

– Old Mother Hubbard <u>went</u> to the cupboard.

A simple sentence can be quite long:

– On the third day of Christmas my true love <u>sent</u> to me, three French hens, two turtle doves and a partridge in a pear tree.

Compound Sentences

Compound sentences have more than one clause. Each clause (underlined in the example below) could be a sentence on its own, but they are joined to make a compound sentence, using the conjunctions *and, but, or*:

– <u>Old Mother Hubbard went to the cupboard</u> but <u>she found that the cupboard was bare</u>.

Complex Sentences

Complex sentences also have more than one clause. The main clause (underlined in the examples below) makes sense on its own. The other clauses depend on the main clause to make sense:

– <u>They all chased after the farmer's wife</u>, who cut off their tails with a carving knife.
– <u>Jack and Jill went up the hill</u> to fetch a pail of water.

The main clause, which makes sense on its own, is not always at the beginning of the sentence. The main clauses (underlined) in the sentences below come at the end of the sentences:

– As I was going to St Ives, <u>I met a man with seven wives</u>.
– When I am king, <u>you shall be queen</u>.

Conditional Sentences

Conditional means 'depending on certain conditions'. Conditional clauses usually contain words such as 'if' or 'unless'. They are used in complex sentences:

– Little Bo Peep will be delighted **if** she finds her sheep.
– Jack's mother will not let him go to the well **unless** he wears a hard hat.

I'll be delighted **if** I find my sheep.

Standard English

Standard English means English which…
- follows all the rules of grammar
- does not include slang
- is pronounced as indicated in English dictionaries.

Non-Standard English

Non-standard English means regional English – different dialects, in which things such as pronunciation and verb forms are different. The table below shows some non-standard forms of English alongside their standard forms.

Non-Standard (Dialectal) Form	Standard Form
They were all <u>sat</u> in the waiting room.	They were all sitting in the waiting room.
I <u>seen</u> him climbing over the wall.	I saw him climbing over the wall.
That's what I <u>does</u>.	That's what I do.
It <u>were</u> cold yesterday.	It was cold yesterday.

Double negatives are used in many regional dialects (non-standard English). A double negative is when two negatives are used when only one is needed, for example…

Non-Standard (Dialectal) Form	Standard Form
I <u>can't</u> get <u>no</u> more of those.	I <u>can't</u> get <u>any</u> more of those.
The house <u>hasn't</u> got <u>no</u> roof.	The house <u>hasn't</u> got <u>a</u> roof.

Non-Standard Word Use

Non-standard word use means using words incorrectly or in an unusual way. Look at the following examples:

Non-Standard Form	Standard Form
It was <u>right</u> cold yesterday.	It was <u>very</u> cold yesterday.
It was a lion <u>what</u> we saw.	It was a lion <u>that</u> we saw.
She wore one of <u>them</u> long coats.	She wore one of <u>those</u> long coats.

Regional Dialect Words

Dialect words (words and meanings unique to that dialect) have developed in different regions:
- 'claggy' is used in Northumberland to mean 'misty and damp'
- 'spice' is used in Yorkshire to mean 'sweets'
- 'kitting' is used in Cornwall to mean 'stealing'.

Worldwide English

English-speaking countries, such as Australia, many African countries, Caribbean countries and the United States, have their own forms of English. People from English-speaking countries understand each other but they use some different words and phrases, different spellings, and have some different rules of grammar.

 Always use Standard English in your writing except where non-standard English creates the effect you want.

Spelling

Using Spellings You Know

When you want to write a word whose spelling you are unsure of, it can be useful to think of other words like it, which you do know how to spell.

Word-Building

You can build longer words from shorter words. If you know what the shorter word means, and how to spell it, this can help you to spell longer words correctly.

Look at the first row in the table below. If you know that 'sign' means a mark or a label, and you know how to spell it, when you need to spell a longer word such as 'signature', you should be able to get at least the first bit (containing 'sign') correct.

Short word	Meaning	Longer Words
sign	mark / label	design, signature, signal
sure	certain	assure, reassure, surely
board	plank, table	cupboard, sideboard, boardroom
weak	not strong	weakling, weaken, weakness
place	site, position	replace, displace, workplace

Word Families

When a number of words are related, they form a **word family**, for example…
- 'family', 'familiar', 'unfamiliar' and 'familiarise' make a word family.
- 'relate', 'relation', 'relative' and 'relatively' make another word family.

Using Mnemonics

Mnemonics are memory aids; they help you to remember things. Mnemonics can help with your spelling. Look at the following list of words, which you may find difficult to spell, and their mnemonics:
- **won**derful – He **won** a wonderful prize.
- te**ache**r – There is an **ache** in teachers because they are a pain!
- **temper**ature – There is a hot **temper** in temperature.
- fri**end** – We will be friends to the **end**.
- **Wed**nesday – They **wed** on Wednesday.

> 💡 Try to make up your own mnemonics to help you remember how to spell words which you find difficult.

sign
signal
design
signature

sure
assure
reassure
surely

Syllables

A syllable is a part of a word that contains a vowel ('a', 'e', 'i', 'o' and 'u') or 'y'. Breaking down long words into syllables makes it easier to spell them. The table below gives some examples.

syll – a – ble

Word	Syllables	Number of Syllables
adjective	ad–ject–ive	3
educational	ed–u–ca–tion–al	5
politician	pol–it–i–cian	4
reporting	re–port–ing	3
paint	paint	1

Phonemes

A phoneme is an individual sound in a word. If you break a word down into its separate phonemes, it can help you to spell it correctly because you are less likely to miss letters out.

Word	Phonemes	Number of Phonemes
clue	c–l–ue	3
computer	c–o–m–p–u–t–er	7
history	h–i–s–t–or–y	6
paint	p–ai–n–t	4
share	sh–are	2

Do not confuse phonemes with syllables. The word 'clue' has one syllable, but it has three phonemes; the word 'sharing' has two syllables, but it has five phonemes.

Words generally have more phonemes than syllables, because a phoneme is a single sound (e.g. 'c', 'l' and 'ue'). A syllable may have a number of these sounds within it (e.g. 'clue').

ph - o - n - e - me

Spelling

Word Derivations

Many words in the English language derive (come) from different languages, especially languages spoken by people who invaded and settled in Britain. The Romans brought Latin, the Normans brought French and the Vikings brought Old Norse. The table below gives some examples.

Word	Language	Meaning	English Words Created
annus	Latin	year	annual, annually
aqua	Latin	water	aquarium, aquatic
locus	Latin	place	location, locate
corps	French	body	corpse
hnakki	Old Norse	nape	neck, necklace

Derivation means the source of a word – where it came from. You can look up the derivation of a word in an etymological dictionary, which will tell you the language it originally came from.

Sometimes, derivations can help to explain unusual spellings, for example…

Old English			Modern English
Cildu ⇒	childer ⇒	childre ⇒	children

Derivations can also help to explain why some words which sound the same, have different meanings and spellings, for example, the words 'wait' and 'weight' in Modern English:

– 'wait' comes from the French 'waiter' meaning 'to wake'.

– 'weight' comes from the Old English '(ge)wiht', meaning 'to weigh'.

Root Words

A root word is a word which can have an extra part attached to the beginning (a prefix) or to the end (a suffix). The table below shows five root words, and some words that can be made by adding a prefix or a suffix to each.

Root Word	Words Formed by Adding a Prefix / Suffix
hill	down<u>hill</u>, up<u>hill</u>, <u>hill</u>side
nation	<u>nation</u>al, <u>nation</u>ality, inter<u>nation</u>al
side	down<u>side</u>, in<u>side</u>, out<u>side</u>, <u>side</u>line
port	ex<u>port</u>, im<u>port</u>, <u>port</u>able
appear	dis<u>appear</u>, dis<u>appear</u>ance, re<u>appear</u>

Prefixes

A prefix is added to the beginning of a root word in order to change its meaning. The spelling of the root word stays the same.

Prefix	+	Root Word	=	New Word
by-	+	pass	=	bypass
over-	+	take	=	overtake
up-	+	stairs	=	upstairs

Some common prefixes are shown in the table.

Prefix	Meaning	Examples
extra-	outside, beyond	extraterrestrial, extraordinary
fore-	before, in front of	foresee, foreground
inter-	among, between	international, intercontinental
multi-	many	multicultural, multicoloured
post-	after	postgraduate, postnatal
pre-	before	premature, prehistoric
re-	(do) again	reuse, rebuild
super-	above, greater	superhuman, supervisor
tri-	three	triangle, tricycle

Negative Prefixes

There are several negative prefixes which have similar meanings. Here are some of the most common ones: *de-, dis-, il-, im-, in-, ir-, non-, un-*.

Some mean exactly the same thing, but they are used in different places according to the letter that the root word begins with. For example, the following prefixes all mean 'not':

- *im-* (before the letters 'b', 'm' or 'p'), e.g. imbalance, immature, impolite
- *il-* (before the letter 'l'), e.g. illegal, illiterate
- *ir-* (before the letter 'r'), e.g. irrational, irregular.

Negative prefixes are sometimes linked to the root word with a hyphen, especially *non-*, as in 'non-appearance', 'non-swimmer', 'non-fiction', etc.

Many negative prefixes mean 'not' or 'no', but they can have slightly different meanings when they are used with the same root word. Look at the table below.

Root Word	Prefix	Negative	Meaning
able	*dis-*	disable	to take away ability
	un-	unable	not able
appearance	*dis-*	disappearance	vanishing
	non-	non-appearance	not appearing or not turning up
connect	*dis-*	disconnected	with a connection or link taken away
	un-	unconnected	not connected, not linked
cover	*dis-*	discover	find something not known to people
	un-	uncover	reveal (something hidden)

Spelling

Suffixes

A suffix can be added to the end of a root word to change its meaning. Adding a suffix could put the word into a different class. For example, it could turn a verb into a noun, a noun into an adjective, or an adjective into a verb.

The table below shows some common suffixes which are added to verbs to form common nouns.

Suffix	Use	Common Noun Formed
-ant	the verb 'inform'	informant
-ee	the verb 'employ'	employee
-er	the verb 'teach'	teacher
-ery	the verb 'brew'	brewery

An abstract noun (a noun which is not a person, object or place) can be formed by adding a suffix to another noun, verb or adjective:

Suffix	Use	Abstract Noun Formed
-age	the verb 'spill'	spillage
-tion	the verb 'collect'	collection
-ism	the noun 'age'	ageism
-ness	the adjective 'useful'	usefulness
-ship	the noun 'friend'	friendship

An adjective can be formed by adding a suffix to a noun:

Suffix	Use	Adjective Formed
-able	the noun 'fashion'	fashionable
-al	the noun 'music'	musical
-ial	the noun 'part'	partial
-ish	the noun 'child'	childish
-less	the noun 'home'	homeless
-y	the noun 'risk'	risky

A verb can be formed by adding a suffix to an adjective or noun:

The verb 'pressurise' is formed from the suffix -ise and the noun 'pressure'.

The verb 'solidify' is formed from the suffix -ify and the adjective 'solid'.

Word-Building with Suffixes

Word-building with *-ion*

When you add the suffix *-ion* to a root word, you might have to change the root word in some way, for example…

- by taking off the final 'e':
  - create ➡ creation
  - revise ➡ revision
- by taking off the final 'e' and adding a new letter(s):
  - compete ➡ competition
  - converse ➡ conversation
- by changing the root word:
  - divide ➡ division
  - solve ➡ solution

Some root words, however, remain the same:

- inspect ➡ inspection
- subtract ➡ subtraction
- invent ➡ invention
- impress ➡ impression

Word-building with *-y*

The letter 'y' acts as a vowel. You can make adjectives by adding *-y* to a root word:

- dream ➡ dreamy
- smell ➡ smelly
- dirt ➡ dirty
- fuss ➡ fussy
- hair ➡ hairy

These root words do not change.

💡 If the root word ends in 'e', this is dropped when the *-y* is added:
- slime ➡ slimy
- shine ➡ shiny
- rose ➡ rosy
- shade ➡ shady

Word-building with *-ly*

Adverbs can be formed by adding the suffix *-ly* to the root word. The root word stays the same:

- fair ➡ fairly
- near ➡ nearly
- quiet ➡ quietly
- main ➡ mainly
- fresh ➡ freshly

Word-building with *-ily*

Adverbs can be formed from adjectives ending in 'y'. Replace the 'y' with the suffix *-ily*:

- dreamy ➡ dreamily
- lucky ➡ luckily
- happy ➡ happily
- cheery ➡ cheerily
- heavy ➡ heavily

Spelling

Changing the Endings of the Root Word

Sometimes, when a suffix is added, the spelling of the root word changes.

If the suffix begins with a consonant (e.g. *-ly*, *-ment*), the spelling of the root word does not usually change:

- brave ➡ **brave**ly
- excite ➡ **excite**ment
- care ➡ **care**ful

If the suffix begins with a vowel (e.g. *-ing*, *-ism*), the spelling of the root word usually changes by dropping the final 'e':

- change ➡ **chang**ing
- inflate ➡ **inflat**able
- race ➡ **rac**ism
- face ➡ **fac**ial

> 💡 Note that some keep the final 'e' in order to keep 'g' or 'c' soft:
> - change ➡ changeable
> - manage ➡ manageable
> - trace ➡ traceable

Doubling the Final Consonant

Double the final consonant (except 'w', 'x' and 'y') before adding a suffix if...

- the suffix begins with a vowel (or *-y*):
  - put ➡ putt**ing**
  - mud ➡ mudd**y**
  - rob ➡ robb**ed**
- the final syllable in the root word is stressed:
  - forbid ➡ forbidden
  - forget ➡ forgettable
  - occur ➡ occurrence

Also double the final consonant in the following words:

- handicap ➡ handicapped
- kidnap ➡ kidnapped
- kidnap ➡ kidnapping
- worship ➡ worshipped
- worship ➡ worshipping

Do not double the final consonant...

- before the suffix *-ic*:
  - acid ➡ acidic
  - poet ➡ poetic
- if the final consonant is 'c'. Instead, add *-k*:
  - picnic ➡ picnickers
  - traffic ➡ trafficking
- if the root word ends in two consonants:
  - bend ➡ be**nd**ing
  - drink ➡ dri**nk**able
- if the suffix begins with a consonant:
  - cheer ➡ cheer**f**ul
  - effort ➡ effort**l**ess

Plurals

The most common way to make a noun plural is to add *-s*, for example...

- apple ➡ apples
- cat ➡ cats
- book ➡ books

Some nouns need an 'e' before the *-s*. This happens when the noun ends with...

- -s, e.g. bus ➡ buses
- -ss, e.g. class ➡ classes
- -x, e.g. fox ➡ foxes
- -sh, e.g. wish ➡ wishes
- -ch, e.g. beach ➡ beaches

An easy way to remember these is if you try to say any of these words with just an 's' at the end to make it plural. They are very difficult to say – boxs, blemishs, classs!

fox

foxes

Plurals of Words Ending in 'o'

The plural of a word ending in 'o' usually just takes -s. Some take -es but, for others, either is correct.

All words ending with two vowels are made plural simply by adding -s.
- kangaroo ➡ kangaroos
- patio ➡ patios
- video ➡ videos

Add -s

dynamos, kilos, kimonos
pianos, ponchos

Add -es

buffaloes, dominoes, echoes,
mosquitoes, potatoes
tomatoes, volcanoes

Add either -s or -es

flamingos / flamingoes
mangos / mangoes
banjos / banjoes

Plurals of Words Ending in 'y'

When a word ends with a vowel and 'y', add -s:
- monkey ➡ monkeys
- tray ➡ trays
- boy ➡ boys

When a word ends with a consonant and 'y', the 'y' becomes 'ie'. We can then just add the usual plural -s:
- baby ➡ babies
- cherry ➡ cherries
- copy ➡ copies
- jelly ➡ jellies

In hyphenated words, the first word is made plural:
- brother-in-law ➡ brothers-in-law
- passer-by ➡ passers-by

Spelling

Plurals of Words Ending in 'f'

If a word ends with 'f' or 'fe' we change the 'f' to 'v' and add -es. If the word ends in 'fe', we still change the 'f' to 'v', but add just -s.

- elf ➡ elves
- half ➡ halves
- loaf ➡ loaves
- shelf ➡ shelves
- thief ➡ thieves
- wife ➡ wives
- wolf ➡ wolves

Note the following exceptions:
- chiefs, handkerchiefs, gulfs, reefs, roofs.

Foreign Plurals

In English, the plurals of many words which have come from other languages can be formed as shown below.

- Words ending 'us', change 'us' to 'i':
  - cactus ➡ cacti
- Words ending 'a', change 'a' to 'ae':
  - formula ➡ formulae
- Words ending 'ex', change 'ex' to 'ices':
  - index ➡ indices
- Words ending 'is', change 'is' to 'es':
  - axis ➡ axes
- Words ending 'on', change 'on' to 'a':
  - criterion ➡ criteria

Irregular Plurals

There are a number of plural forms which have no pattern. You just have to learn them!

- foot ➡ feet
- goose ➡ geese
- tooth ➡ teeth
- man ➡ men
- woman ➡ women
- child ➡ children
- ox ➡ oxen
- mouse ➡ mice
- die ➡ dice

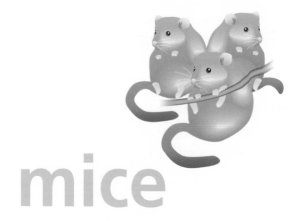

Words with No Plural

Some words have no plural, for example…
- words for materials in bulk:
  - aluminium, brass, cocoa, coffee, concrete, honey, rice, tea, treacle
- words for subjects or topics:
  - chemistry, geography, biology
- abstract nouns:
  - eternity, happiness, intelligence, ugliness
- some animals and fish:
  - deer, sheep, cod, haddock, salmon.

Silent Letters

Many English words contain 'silent' letters. These are letters which are not pronounced. Most of these can be traced to the derivations of the words, when the silent letter(s) would have been pronounced. For example, 'gnaw' is from Old English *gnagan* (to gnaw).

The most common silent letters in English are shown below.

Silent Letter	Examples
b	bomb, climb, comb, crumb, numb, plumber, limb, debt
c	ascertain, discipline, muscle, scent, sceptre
d	handsome, handkerchief
g	gnome, sign, reign, campaign, foreign
h	hour, ghost, rhythm, shepherd, exhaust, honest, heir
k	knife, knock, knuckle, know, knit, knee
l	yolk, folk, salmon, could, should, would
n	autumn, hymn, column, solemn
s	aisle, isle, island, debris
t	soften, listen, castle, whistle
w	answer, wrap, wrist, two, write, wrong

Many words contain a silent 'gh', for example…
- **igh** words: fight, high, night, sigh, slight
- **ough** words: bough, drought, plough, although, dough, though, bought, brought, fought, ought, sought
- **augh** words: daughter, naughty, slaughter
- **eigh** and **aigh** words: eight, freight, height, weight, neighbour, straight.

In some words, 'gh' is pronounced like an 'f', for example…
- cough, enough, laughter, rough, tough.

Unstressed Vowels

The vowels are a, e, i, o and u. Unstressed vowels are…
- vowels which are not pronounced (e.g. the second 'e' in temperature)
- vowels which are pronounced 'uh' in an unstressed syllable (e.g. the first 'o' in alcohol).

Each of the words below contains a vowel which is not pronounced at all. The coloured versions show how we pronounce the words; the unstressed vowels are marked by the apostrophes.

- cemetery — cemet'ry
- stationery — station'ry
- different — diff'rent
- factory — fact'ry
- interesting — int'resting

The words below contain unstressed vowels that are pronounced 'uh'. The coloured versions show how we pronounce the words; the unstressed vowels are marked '-uh-'.

- calendar — calend-uh
- slipper — slip-uh
- underground — und-uh-ground

 Be careful when you spell words with unstressed vowels. Make sure you don't miss the vowel out. Try to learn the spelling for words which have vowels pronounced 'uh'.

ssshhh

Spelling

Homonyms, Homographs and Homophones

These are all words which are easily confused.

Homonym means 'same name'. Homonyms are words which are spelled the same and pronounced the same, but they might have different meanings. For example…
- bow (rhyming with 'glow' – a weapon for firing arrows)
- bow (rhyming with 'glow' – a fancy knot).

Homograph means 'same writing'. Homographs are words which are spelled the same but might be pronounced differently. For example…
- bow (rhyming with 'glow' – a weapon for firing arrows)
- bow (rhyming with 'cow' – to bend forward).

Homophone means 'same sound'. Homophones are words which sound the same but might be spelled differently. For example…
- bow (rhyming with 'cow' – to bend forward)
- bough (rhyming with 'cow' – a branch of a tree).

Here is a list of homophones. Make sure you know the difference between the words in each pair so that you don't use the wrong ones in your writing.

air (mixture of gases)	heir (someone who inherits)
allowed (let)	aloud (able to be heard)
cereal (food crop)	serial (a series)
coarse (rough)	course (route / series of lessons)
fair (just / light-coloured / festival)	fare (money paid by a passenger)
hole (gap, ditch)	whole (entire)
pane (sheet of glass)	pain (ache)
sail (canvas on a boat)	sale (selling things)
stationary (still)	stationery (paper, etc.)
threw (past tense of throw)	through (from one side to the other)
throne (ceremonial chair)	thrown (past tense of throw)
where (in what place?)	wear (e.g. a coat)

See if you can think of other examples.

Noun and Verb Homophones

Some nouns sound the same as the verbs they come from, but note that they are spelled differently.

Verb	Noun
license	licence
practise	practice

Some nouns sound slightly different to the verbs they come from.

Verb	Noun
advise	advice

 Remember, nouns take 'c'. Verbs take 's'. For example:
- I need some advi**c**e. (noun)
- I will advi**s**e you about any changes. (verb)

Tricky Words

Words can be difficult to spell for different reasons, as we have seen.

This page lists some tricky words that do not follow any spelling patterns. You just have to learn them!

Difficult Vowels

This table lists some vowel sounds that can be produced by different spellings:

Vowel	Examples
short 'a'	ch**a**t, pl**ai**t
long 'a'	d**ay**, r**ai**n, **ei**ght, ob**ey**, gr**ea**t
short 'e'	b**e**d, br**ea**d, fri**e**nd, l**ei**sure, s**ai**d, **a**ny
long 'e'	m**ee**t, m**ea**t, p**ie**ce, l**e**gal, c**ei**ling
short 'i'	**i**n, w**o**men, s**ie**ve, forf**ei**t, pr**e**tty, s**y**stem, b**ui**ld, b**u**siness
long 'i'	p**i**ne, s**ig**n, sk**y**, h**ei**ght, b**uy**, **ai**sle
short 'o'	c**o**t, w**a**sh, c**ou**gh
long 'o'	b**oa**t, s**ew**, t**oe**, h**o**le, th**ou**gh
short 'u'	c**u**t, c**ou**ntry, fl**oo**d, w**o**man
'oo'	s**oo**n, s**ou**p, bl**ue**, sh**oe**, br**ui**se, t**u**ne
'or'	rep**or**t, b**a**ll, fl**oor**, s**aw**, w**ar**m, **au**thor, y**our**, **oar**
'air'	**air**, h**eir**, sh**are**, v**ar**y, **aer**ial

Difficult Consonants

This table lists some consonant sounds that can be produced by different spellings:

Consonant	Examples
'b'	a**b**out, a**bb**reviation
hard 'c'/'k'	**c**ut, sa**ck**, a**ch**e, bi**ke**
soft 'c'/'s'	practi**c**e, practi**s**e, fu**ss**
hard 's'/'z'	ri**s**e, bu**zz**, ra**z**or
'sh'	**sh**ut, ra**ci**al, por**tio**n, controver**si**al
'ch'	**ch**at, ma**tch**
hard 'g'	**g**o, a**gg**ravate
'j' or soft 'g'	in**j**ure, a**g**e, ba**dg**er

Sometimes it helps to think of the spellings of words from the same root (see page 16).

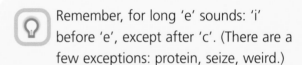 Remember, for long 'e' sounds: 'i' before 'e', except after 'c'. (There are a few exceptions: protein, seize, weird.)

"My bl**ue** sh**oe** gave me a br**ui**se"

Reading Fiction

Genre

Most stories belong to a **genre**. A genre is a category of writing, for example, *Alice's Adventures in Wonderland* by Lewis Carroll belongs to the **fantasy** genre. Some genres and their typical features are given below. There are many more.

romance *(love stories)*
- emotional words associated with romance, e.g. kiss
- a boy and a girl meeting and falling in love
- attractive setting / surroundings.

ACTION & ADVENTURE
- treasure, maps, discoveries
- an explorer, the hero
- exotic setting, e.g. jungle, mountains, caves.

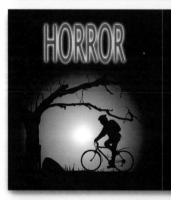

HORROR
- spooky words, e.g. dark, creepy, shiver
- creatures, ghosts, monsters
- scary setting, e.g. dark forests at night, castles.

SCIENCE FICTION
- robots, aliens, spacemen
- space and different planets
- unusual, sometimes made-up, words and names for planets, aliens etc.

The Narrator

All stories are told by a narrator. As well as telling the story, the narrator…
- sets the scene
- tells the reader about the characters.

The narrator of a story will be the author or one of the characters.

If the author is the narrator, the story is written in the third person (he, she, him, her, they, them), as in the passage below.

> Katy's heart gave a great thump, but she rose bravely: 'I made up the game, and I was Father Ocean,' she said to the astonished Mrs Knight, who… replied solemnly, 'Very well, Katy – sit down,' which Katy did, feeling more ashamed than ever, but somehow relieved in her mind.
>
> from *What Katy Did* by Susan Coolidge

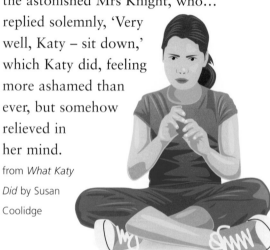

If one of the characters is the narrator, the story is written in the first person (I, me, we, us), as in the passage below.

> I hand the first book to mother. Perhaps it is a grammar, perhaps a history, or geography. I take a last drowning look at the page as I give it into her hand, and start off aloud at a racing pace while I have got it fresh. I trip over a word. Mr Murdstone looks up. I trip over another word. Miss Murdstone looks up. I redden, tumble over half-a-dozen words, and stop.
>
> from *David Copperfield* by Charles Dickens

Points of View

Sometimes authors do not just tell a story; they communicate a point of view or opinion. Sometimes, this may be a very simple, small point, which is communicated very clearly, for example…

> Back then, it was the norm to leave the front door unlocked when we left the house – and the windows wide open to let in the fresh air. Back then, we didn't need to think twice.

The author is communicating to us that people felt safer in the past.

Sometimes the author expresses something which might be an opinion, or it might be an idea to get us thinking, for example…

> Everyone knows that fairies exist. Otherwise, how do all the little miracles take place?

Here the author communicates an idea as if it were a fact.

Sometimes, an author communicates his or her opinions to us in a less obvious way, such as through what happens to the characters in the story.

For example, a story set in a school might have a mean character who bullies other children. The consequence might be something going wrong for the mean character, or he or she might change and become a nicer person.

The message would be that bullying is wrong and that it has unpleasant consequences, unless it stops.

Look out for opinions and messages given in a story. Think about what the story is really telling you.

Reading Fiction

Stories from Different Times

A story from the past is a story which was written a long time ago. This is not the same as a story *about* the past. A story *about* the past may have been written very recently.

It is quite easy to tell the difference between a story from the past and a modern story by looking at the vocabulary and grammar.

Vocabulary

New words are always coming into the English language, whilst others drop out of use or change their meaning. The table below gives some examples.

Old Vocabulary	Modern Vocabulary
abode	home
hitherto	until now
thrice	three times
thee	you
hence	so / therefore

Grammar

Modern English uses more **contractions** (abbreviated words) than older English:

Old Form	Modern Form
Did he not?	Didn't he?
Do they not?	Don't they?
Should he not?	Shouldn't he?
Will you not?	Won't you?

Exclamations have also changed over time. Few people now say *Golly!*, *By Jove!*, *Mercy!* or *Good gracious!* to express their surprise, or *Fiddlesticks!* or *Balderdash!* to mean nonsense or rubbish.

Note that a story written recently could use old vocabulary and grammar to tell a story about the past.

Stories from Different Places

Stories from different places are set in different countries or different cultures.

Very often, the authors who write these stories are from that country or are part of that culture.

In these stories we often find different points of view, as well as different settings.

We also find different vocabulary and styles of language, for example, non-standard (regional) English from different parts of Britain and from other countries.

 When you are reading stories, look for clues that tell you when and where they are set, such as the language used, the characters' behaviour and events which would not happen nowadays or would not happen in places you know.

'How old are you, Topsy?'

'Dun no, Missis,' said the image, with a grin that showed all her teeth.

'Don't know how old you are? Didn't anybody ever tell you? Who was your mother?'

'Never had none!' said the child, with another grin.

'Never had any mother? What do you mean? Where were you born?'

'Never was born!' persisted Topsy, with another grin, that looked so goblin-like, that, if Miss Ophelia had been at all nervous, she might have fancied that she had got hold of some sooty gnome from the land of Diablerie; but Miss Ophelia was not nervous, but plain and business-like, and she said, with some sternness, 'You mustn't answer me in that way, child; I'm not playing with you. Tell me where you were born, and who your father and mother were.'

'Never was born,' reiterated the creature, more emphatically; 'never had no father nor mother, nor nothin'. I was raised by a speculator, with lots of others. Old Aunt Sue used to take car on us.'

The child was evidently sincere, and Jane, breaking into a short laugh, said, 'Laws, Missis, there's heaps of 'em. Speculators buys 'em up cheap, when they's little, and gets 'em raised for market.'

from *Uncle Tom's Cabin* by Harriet Beecher Stowe

Uncle Tom's Cabin, by Harriet Beecher Stowe, is a story from a different time and place. It is set in the southern states of America at a time when slavery was legal (before 1865). A little black girl called Topsy has been bought from a speculator (slave dealer) and given to Miss Ophelia.

The characters' language and their attitudes show where and when it is set. It tells us that…
- black slaves could be bought from dealers
- dealers bought slaves when they were very young and raised them like farmers raise animals, before selling them on to make money.

In the final paragraph, Jane's words tell us that…
- children bought as slaves rarely knew who their parents were
- slave children had to work; they were not educated.

The passage shows the type of English spoken by Topsy and Jane (see tables alongside).

Feature of Non-Standard English	Examples from Topsy and Jane	Standard English Version
Double negatives	Never had none nor nothin'	Never had any Nor anything
Non-agreement	Speculator<u>s</u> <u>buys</u>' em up when <u>they's</u> little	Speculator<u>s</u> <u>buy</u> them up when <u>they're</u> little

Spellings which show Non-Standard Pronunciation	Standard Pronunciation
dun no nothin' take car on us 'em	don't know nothing take care of us them

Reading Fiction

Language for Effect

Authors use language to help the reader to picture the scene. The language used can create an atmosphere such as…

- humour
- disgust
- excitement
- mystery
- fear
- horror
- suspense.

Authors choose words to create these effects. They think about…

- nouns
- adjectives
- verbs
- adverbs.

> Laurel skipped down the lane, picking at the flowers as she passed. On reaching the cottage, she flung the gate open and, without stopping to close it behind her, bounded up the stone path to the front door.

The verbs used in this passage communicate happiness and excitement: Laurel is pleased to arrive at the cottage. Think about the different effect the passage would have if the highlighted verbs were changed to 'stomped', 'kicked' and 'stamped'.

Figurative Language

Figurative language means when people, places or objects are compared to, or described as if they were, something else. Three important types of figurative language are as follows:

Comparisons (similes) – compare something to something else, and often contain 'as' or 'like', for example…

- His clothes were like old rags.
- Her voice was as loud as a foghorn.

Metaphors – say something *is* something else, for example…

- Chloe's bedroom is a pig-sty.
- I ate a mountain of mashed potato.

Personification – makes an object seem human, for example…

- The clouds hugged the mountain tops.
- The fingers of the tree pulled at my hair.

> The rain was torrential, battering relentlessly on the roof of the car. The sky had become a thick dark blanket which seemed to engulf us menacingly. There was nothing we could do except wait, so we huddled up together in frightened silence.

This passage uses adjectives and adverbs to create an atmosphere of suspense and fear. This helps us to picture the scene. The author has thought carefully about the verbs used, and the passage contains an effective metaphor.

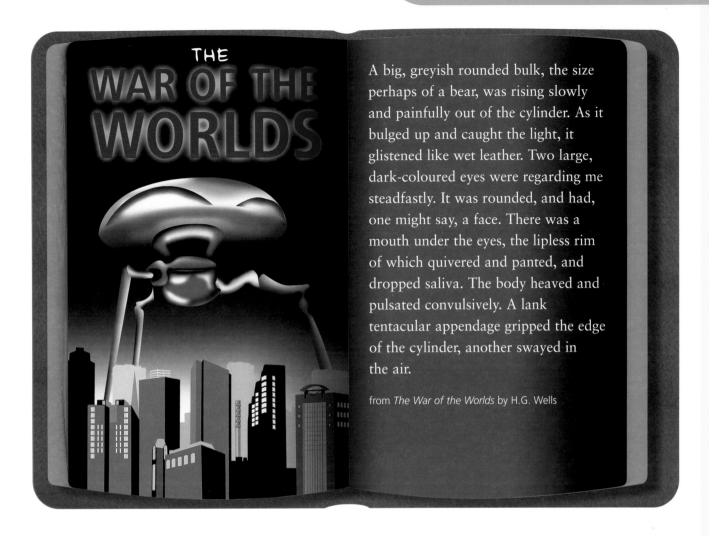

A big, greyish rounded bulk, the size perhaps of a bear, was rising slowly and painfully out of the cylinder. As it bulged up and caught the light, it glistened like wet leather. Two large, dark-coloured eyes were regarding me steadfastly. It was rounded, and had, one might say, a face. There was a mouth under the eyes, the lipless rim of which quivered and panted, and dropped saliva. The body heaved and pulsated convulsively. A lank tentacular appendage gripped the edge of the cylinder, another swayed in the air.

from *The War of the Worlds* by H.G. Wells

Atmosphere

The passage above, from *The War of the Worlds* by H.G. Wells, uses language to create a feeling of horror. It does this by describing the alien bit by bit, and in detail, as it emerges from the spaceship.

- The nouns help us to picture the alien.
- The adjectives and comparisons help us to imagine the horror of the scene.
- The verbs create a picture of how the alien moves.
- The adverbs tell us more about how the alien comes into view and how it moves.

Words and phrases which help to create a feeling of terror, horror and revulsion are listed here:

Verbs / Verb Phrases	rising, bulged, glistened, regarding, dropped saliva, quivered, panted, heaved, pulsated, gripped, swayed
Adverbs	slowly, painfully, steadfastly

Nouns	bulk, eyes, face, mouth, appendage
Adjectives	big, greyish, rounded, large, dark-coloured, lank, tentacular
Comparisons	the size perhaps of a bear, like wet leather

Writers can use language to make readers like or dislike characters, or sympathise with them. When reading many fairy stories, such as *Jack and the Beanstalk*, you probably thought of the giants as bad characters but if you have read *The BFG* by Roald Dahl you probably felt very fond of the BFG.

 Think about how the language used makes you feel about the characters.

Reading Fiction

Responding

When you are asked to respond to a story that you have read, you could think about the following:

- What the story is about, its genre, and when and where it is set.
- Any messages and opinions it might contain.
- Descriptions of characters, events and places – what do they tell you?
- The type of language that has been used and why.
- The effects created by the language.
- The effects created by illustrations (if any are included).
- How the story affects you.

> Read the story carefully before you try to respond to it. You will be asked to back up your answers with evidence from the story. For example, if you are asked what a character is like, you could support your answer by quoting a short piece of text or by describing an event in the text.

Example

Sabrina knocked on the door and stepped back to wait patiently for an answer. After a couple of minutes, Mrs Johnson opened the door and peered around it, squinting through her thick glasses.

'Is that you, Sabrina?' she enquired quietly.

'Yes it's me, Mrs Johnson,' Sabrina replied, 'I've brought you your shopping, and these lovely flowers.'

Sabrina gave the beautifully scented bunch of flowers to the old lady, who smiled with warmth and gratitude. She thanked Sabrina and welcomed her inside, delighted that this kind girl had come to visit again.

1 What sort of character is Sabrina?
Sabrina is patient and kind.

2 How do the events in the story show us this?
She knocks at the door and waits patiently for an answer. She takes some shopping and flowers to the old lady.

3 Give one word from the story which describes Sabrina's character.
Kind.

Types of Non-Fiction

Non-fiction is about real people, places and events. Non-fiction is written to inform, explain, persuade, advise, argue, describe, etc.

There are many types of non-fiction. Some are described here.

Biographies and Autobiographies

A biography is the story of a person's life written by someone else in the third person ('he', 'she', 'it', etc.).

The word 'biography' comes from the Greek *bios* (life) and *graphos* (written) – so biography means 'written life'. The writer chooses the parts of a person's life to write about and informs readers about what the person said and did.

An autobiography is a life story written by the person himself / herself in the first person ('I', 'me', etc.). Writers share their thoughts, ideas and feelings but, unlike in a biography, they are not interpreted by someone else.

Auto is a Greek word meaning 'self' – so autobiography means 'self-written life'.

If you think about the derivation of the words biography and autobiography you will remember which is which.

Diaries

Some autobiographies are written as diaries. They might not have been written for publication. For example, *The Diary of a Young Girl* by Anne Frank, was written by a Jewish girl whose family hid from the Nazis during the Second World War.

Diaries are written for the writer himself / herself. Some writers address their diary as if it were a person (Anne Frank called her diary 'Kitty').

Letters

A letter is a piece of writing addressed to one person, group of people or organisation. A letter can be formal or informal and its purpose might be to…

- send good wishes
- congratulate
- give news or information
- offer sympathy (e.g. if someone has died)
- ask for information or help
- complain.

Notes, Emails and Text Messages

A note is a very short, informal letter.

An email is like a note. It is usually short, and text, photographs, sounds or videos can be attached to it.

Text messages are usually very short. They contain abbreviations and can have text, photographs, sounds or videos attached.

Notes, emails and text messages are used for some of the same purposes as letters.

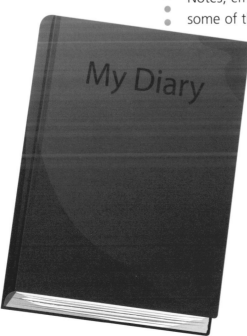

My Diary

don't forget to buy milk

Reading Non-Fiction

Leaflets

A leaflet gives facts and information, often with pictures. It may contain bullet points, colour, illustrations, etc. It might be written to give facts or details (e.g. about a forthcoming event), or it might set out to persuade the reader to do something (e.g. to visit somewhere).

Official Documents

Official documents use very exact language to set out details. Examples of official documents include...

- legal agreements
- forms
- rules and regulations (e.g. rules for competitions)
- contracts (e.g. contracts of employment).

Recounts

A recount is about an event from the past (hours, minutes, days, weeks, months or years ago). It may...

- tell a true story
- report news (see newspaper reports)
- report an eye-witness account
- record the main events of an occasion such as a ceremony or a meeting.

Newspaper Reports / Articles

A newspaper report gives information about an event that has already happened. It might contain...

- an interesting, shocking or amusing headline
- sub-headings which make the reader want to know more
- quotations (what people have said about the event)
- an eye-catching photo.

Discussions

Discussions give different opinions about an issue and consider one opinion against another. Discussions are presented as arguments. They have an introduction to the issue, and a conclusion which summarises both opinions (see also page 69).

Examples of current discussions in the news include...

- the pros and cons of wind energy
- what the minimum wage should be
- how recycling can be increased.

Advertisements

Adverts are designed to make people remember a product, service or idea. They aim to persuade people to do something through catchy slogans using humour, plays on words, alliteration and rhyme (see pages 49–50).

Non-Chronological Reports

A non-chronological report can be about a person, a group of people, a place, a situation, or an ongoing event. It is organised according to topic, and may contain descriptions, examples, evidence and proof. A non-chronological report could be…

- a report about a scientific discovery
- information about a local situation such as a dangerous road
- a report about a school.

Read this example of a non-chronological report. It is organised according to topic: the first paragraph tells us about the village of Glozel in general; the second paragraph tells us about the discovery made in the village; the final paragraph tells us about the villager who made the discovery.

Glozel

It has a timeless air of antiquated French rural charm, this place. It is called Glozel, a tiny hamlet – barely a hamlet, even, only a 'locality' – not far from Vichy, nestling in a sheltered hollow in a patchwork of fields and woodlands in the foothills of the Auvergne mountains. Little has changed, one feels, for years and years.

Some seventy years ago, it was the setting for an astonishing discovery – in a field, which is now known as 'The Field of the Dead'. A narrow path leading to the site is hemmed in by trees and electrified fences and punctuated with homemade gates fashioned from old bedsteads. It plunges steeply towards the famous field – a D-shaped clearing, slightly under a hectare in area, with ankle-deep grass carpeted with wild flowers. In the field are two oval hollows: overgrown shallow pits outlined with small rough boulders – the tombs where, in 1924, Emile Fradin and his grandfather dug up hundreds of ancient pots, urns, masks and more…

Back at the farmhouse, Emile Fradin is waiting at the door, still looking every inch the farmer. Beside him is the entrance to the tiny museum he set up in his front room to display the finds. A notice declares 'Musée de Glozel. Entrée 3 Euros' (Glozel Museum. Admission 3 Euros).

adapted from *Fakers, Forgers and Phoneys* by Magnus Magnusson

      Descriptions

      Evidence and proof

Reading Non-Fiction

Scanning

You do not always need to read a text from beginning to end to see if it will tell you what you want to know. You can scan it by…

- looking for clues on the front cover of books, leaflets, etc. in the title, the pictures and any other text
- looking for key words and phrases on the contents page or index (if it has them)
- looking at the pictures
- checking for key words and phrases in the picture captions.

Scanning also helps to give you an overview about the text. For example, whether it is written for an expert in a subject or for someone who does not know a lot about it. You should notice…

- whether the pages are big or small and how many pages there are
- whether the font is big or small
- whether it is mainly text or mainly pictures
- the type of language used
- how interesting it looks.

Skimming

Skimming means reading quickly to find out what a chapter, page or paragraph is about.

You might want to read an information book for enjoyment. But, if you are reading it to find certain information, it may be a waste of time to read every word. You can skim to find the parts you need and then read just these parts in detail.

Sub-headings and quotations in boxes can tell you what a page is about.

Scanning and skimming can be useful with all types of texts – letters, leaflets, newspaper reports, etc.

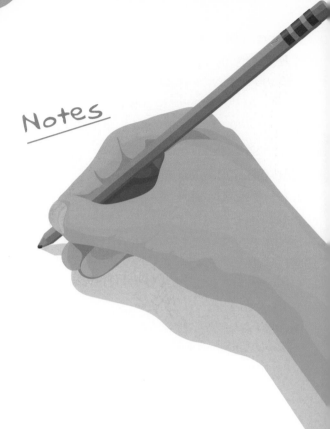

Notes

Making Notes

If you make notes as you read you are more likely to remember the key points of a text. Making notes helps you to summarise the information you have read. This means that you can express it in your own words when you write about the topic.

To note the key points of a text you should…

- write words and phrases (not complete sentences)
- write important words clearly and in full so that you know how to spell them
- use arrows and lines to help you to link points
- use abbreviations such as these:

and	+ **or** &
describe / description	desc.
hours	hrs
less than	<
minutes	mins
more than	>
number	no.
road	rd
seconds	secs
square	sq.
therefore	∴
years	yrs

Purpose

The purpose of a text is the reason why it was written.

Every piece of non-fiction writing has a purpose, for example…
- to amuse or entertain
- to inform
- to recount (summarise an event)
- to instruct (e.g. give directions)
- to persuade (to convince readers to do something)
- to describe (e.g. a place or event)
- to explain (e.g. how to do something)
- to give different opinions on a subject.

Audience

All texts are written for a particular audience. The audience is the people the author had in mind when he / she wrote the text. For example…
- a children's encyclopaedia is written for an audience of children
- a book on gardening is written for an audience of people interested in gardening
- a leaflet on things to do in Cornwall is written for an audience of people who either live in Cornwall or who plan to visit Cornwall.

Read the following texts:

> With a fantastic play area for the kids, a traditional country pub five minutes away, and glorious surrounding scenery, Greenton Valley campsite is the perfect destination for a relaxing family holiday in the dales.

The **purpose** of this text is to **inform** the audience what the campsite is like and where it is, and perhaps to **persuade** the audience to stay there.

The **audience** of this text is **families** – especially **parents with young children** – who want to go on holiday. We know this because it mentions 'a fantastic play area for the kids' and 'perfect destination for a relaxing family holiday'.

> From junction 25, turn left at the roundabout, and continue for 2 miles. When you cross over the bridge and enter the village, take the second right. The hotel is on the left.

The **purpose** of this text is to **instruct** the audience on how to reach the hotel.

The **audience** of this text is **people who are visiting the hotel**. The audience must also be **drivers**, because the instructions explain how to get to the hotel by road.

When you are reading non-fiction, try to work out the purpose of the text, and the audience it is aimed at. This will help you to understand it.

Reading Non-Fiction

Formal and Informal Language

Formal language is used in official documents and letters, and in notices. Some parts of newspapers are written in formal language (see example bottom right).

Most radio and television news reports and documentaries are in formal language. Spoken formal language is used in ceremonies, speeches and announcements.

Formal language is used mainly between people who do not know one another or where the writer or speaker is addressing a large group of people.

Informal language is used in emails, notes, text messages and some adverts. Some magazines and newspapers use informal language.

Everyday speech is informal language. Informal language is used between people who know one another.

The table below lists the characteristics of formal and informal language.

Formal Language	Informal Language
Impersonal – uses **third person** (he, she, it, they)	**Personal** – uses **first** (I, we), **second** (you) and **third person**
Mainly **passive voice**	Mainly **active voice**
Full words (do not, cannot, etc.)	Many **contractions** (don't, can't, etc.)
Standard English	Some **non-standard English**
Longer sentences	**Shorter sentences**
Complex, specialist vocabulary (see opposite)	**Simple**, everyday vocabulary

Person

A text can be written in the first, second or third person. You can tell which from the pronouns used:

	First Person	Second Person	Third Person
Singular	I, me, my, mine	you, your, yours	he, she, it, his, her, hers
Plural	we, us, our, ours	you, your, yours	they, their, theirs

Vocabulary

Vocabulary means the words used in speech or text. You can use a dictionary or thesaurus to find different words with similar meanings. Some are used in informal speech and writing; others are more formal. For example…

Formal Vocabulary	Informal Vocabulary
applaud	clap
cease	end, stop
consequently	so
furthermore	and
prudent	careful
purchase	buy

When you are reading a non-fiction text, look out for clues that tell you whether it is formal or informal. Think about why formal or informal language has been used.

STORM HAVOC!

Last night's storm caused havoc throughout the local area. Many homes are now without electricity, whilst others have experienced some minor flooding.

Two roads have been closed off due to fallen trees, resulting in heavy traffic jams during this morning's rush hour.

The village of Oakton in particular has been affected with more than 100 homes now without electricity. Electricity companies say they hope to have all local homes reconnected within the next 24 hours.

Fact and Opinion

A fact is a piece of information that can be checked and proven. An opinion is what someone thinks.

Both facts and opinions are found in non-fiction texts, depending on the type of text. For example, a non-chronological report or a set of instructions contains mainly facts, whilst a persuasive text or argument contains opinions.

Some Facts

- Spiders have eight legs.
- Liverpool Football Club won the 2006 FA Cup.
- The island of Lindisfarne is also known as Holy Island.

Some Opinions

- Spiders are horrible creepy crawlies.
- Steven Gerrard's goal was brilliant – a superb shot.
- Lindisfarne is a beautiful island and a wonderful place to relax.

In non-fiction texts, opinions are sometimes expressed as if they are facts, for example…

- It is a very good computer.
- Pepe Reina is the best goalkeeper in the world.
- School-days are the happiest days of your life.

Opinions are used in advertisements to persuade readers to buy the product, for example…

- The freshest taste at the best price!

The adjectives 'freshest' and 'best' are opinions, rather than facts.

Read this passage (written around the beginning of the 20th century) about the first British explorations of Australia in the early 19th century. It contains both facts and opinions.

> The natives were a problem. They were the strangest and most primitive of peoples – savages… wielding a marvellous weapon – the boomerang – and able to make fire by rubbing wood on wood, yet too ignorant to build a hut. They were matchless as climbers and trackers, but generally beast-like in their habits and filled with superstitions and terrors.
>
> The natives, indeed, played their part with us in the opening up of this mighty land of which they had not made any particle of use. Escaping convicts treated them with fearful cruelty at times, and so kindled a vengeful spirit in them.
>
> Yet these poor creatures could be affectionate and faithful. All the big exploring trips included natives, and great things these poor people did at times; terrible things, too, often.

from *The Children's Encyclopedia* edited by Arthur Mee (written at the beginning of the 20th century)

Fact   Opinion

Reading Non-Fiction

Language

The language used in non-fiction texts depends on...
- the text type (e.g. biography, letter, advert)
- its purpose (e.g. to persuade, to instruct)
- the audience (e.g. children, parents).

A formal style is used much more in non-fiction texts than an informal style, although you may come across informal styles in texts like diaries and adverts.

Types of Sentences

Commands (imperatives) tell the reader what to do. They are useful in advertisements, for example...
- Buy it now!
- Come along tomorrow.

Questions are often used in adverts, newspaper articles and leaflets to grab the reader's attention, for example...
- Where would you like to go this summer?

Some questions are **rhetorical questions.** These are questions that do not need answers. For example...
- Why go anywhere else?
- How would you like it?

Simple sentences are often used in leaflets and instructions because they are clear and easy to follow.

Complex and **compound sentences** are often used in descriptions. They can communicate ideas as well as information in a text which does not need to be read quickly.

Read the two non-fiction texts on this page. There is a big difference between these texts, and it is not only because of the subject.

The official document is formal. It uses mostly passive sentences, technical vocabulary and the third person.

The advert is informal. It uses active sentences, everyday vocabulary and it speaks directly to the reader using the second person (you). It also contains commands and a rhetorical question to introduce it.

An Official Document

Competition Rules

The first correct entry drawn after the closing date wins four nights' accommodation for two at the Hotel Swish, Benidorm, Spain.

Entries must be submitted on an official entry form.

Illegible entries shall be declared invalid.

The prize is subject to availability.

The prize is not transferable and there are no cash alternatives.

The publishers accept no liability for losses or injuries suffered in connection with the prize.

	Third person
	Formal language and technical vocabulary
	Passive sentence

An Advert

WHY GET LEFT BEHIND?

FANTASTIC PHONE DEAL

SIGN UP TODAY FOR THE BEST DEAL EVER

You'll love the funky fashion fascias.

Choose your favourite colour and pattern

	Alliteration
	Informal language and everyday vocabulary
	Imperatives (commands)
	Rhetorical question

There may be a number of
HEADINGS

The actual text can be in different
colours and SIZES and can also be
bold, *italic* or <u>underlined</u> or in
• bullet points

Format and Presentation

Format means how the text appears; whether it is handwritten, printed or electronic or whether it is meant to be spoken.

Presentation means what the text looks like. For printed and handwritten texts this includes...

- layout, e.g. one column or more, font style and size, use of tables and borders
- highlighting (bold, italic, underlining)
- use of colour
- illustrations such as photographs, drawings, diagrams, graphs and charts
- headings and sub-headings.

Non-fiction texts often use tables, bullet points, columns and borders. These split up the text, helping to present the information clearly and making it quick and easy to find.

- Headings help readers to find information and to see at a glance what the page is about. They also help to make a page look more interesting.
- Photographs and captions communicate information and make a page look attractive.
- Diagrams help to explain difficult ideas.
- Maps, graphs and charts can help to display information clearly.
- Cartoons, sketches and drawings can add humour or create a friendly, informal effect.

When you read non-fiction texts, think about why certain pictures, colours, font sizes, etc. have been used. Ask yourself questions like 'Do the tables make the information clearer?', 'Do the diagrams help me to understand?', 'Do the pictures grab my interest?'

Reading Non-Fiction

Responding

When you are asked to respond to a non-fiction text which you have read, you should think about the following:

- What the text is about – its subject.
- The purpose of the text.
- The audience and how suitable the text is for that audience.
- Which parts are fact and which parts are opinion.
- The format.
- The presentation features used and the effect they create.
- The language used and the effect it creates – figurative language, direct language, tone, etc.
- How it affects you.

Read the text carefully before you try to respond to it. You will be asked to back up your answers. For example, if you are asked to identify the audience of a text, you might say that it is for young children. You could give as evidence short sentences, simple vocabulary and pictures. You could quote or describe some of these.

Example

Say no to new supermarket!

Supermarket giant Gynormus is planning to build a new superstore in our town.

Some residents say they are pleased about the proposed store because of its low prices and the range of goods that will be available – not only food, but electrical goods, clothes and household items too.

But others are not so welcoming. If Gynormus muscles its way into our community, other shops will close, leaving only Gynormus. Does that offer choice?

Planners say that Gynormus will bring more shoppers into the town from surrounding areas. This is not true – granted, more people will come to shop at this out-of-town site, but they will not venture into the town centre. It is too far away to bring any benefit of this kind.

There will be a planning meeting at the Town Hall on Wednesday 16th August. We urge you to come along and support your town's traders.

1 What is the purpose of this text?
a) To persuade readers to support the building of the supermarket. ☐
b) To describe the supermarket to the readers. ☐
c) To inform the readers about the name of the supermarket. ☐
d) To persuade readers to oppose (be against) the building of the supermarket. ☑

2 Provide an example from the text that shows this, and explain why it shows this.

'Say No to New Supermarket!' This command is telling the readers to oppose the new supermarket.

Poetic Form

Poetic form means the structure of a poem. This depends on…

- the number of lines in the poem
- rhythm and rhyme pattern (see pages 48–49)
- the shape of the poem.

Poets still use traditional poetic forms because they have been found to work well. But, they also create new forms. There are many different types of poems. Some are described here:

A **limerick** is a humorous poem which follows a set pattern:

- It has five lines.
- The first four lines rhyme in sets of two (couplets), i.e. lines 1 and 2 rhyme, and lines 3 and 4 rhyme.
- The fifth line rhymes with the first two.

A **riddle** is a puzzle written in the form of a rhyme. A common type of riddle is one which gives clues for each letter of a word.

A **parody** is a poem which imitates another poem. It uses the rhythm and rhyme patterns of the original poem and sometimes uses words from the original poem. It is often humorous.

A **sonnet** is a very old form of poem. A sonnet has 14 lines. The first 12 are arranged in three sets of four. Each set has alternate lines rhyming. The last two lines are a rhyming couplet. (William Shakespeare wrote many sonnets.)

A **cinquain** has five lines, and a total of 22 syllables. The last line often adds something unexpected to give the poem impact.

A **clerihew** has four lines in two rhyming couplets. The subject is named in the first line. A clerihew is usually about people, but can be about animals or non-living things.

A **haiku** is an old form of poem from Japan. It has 17 syllables in three lines. The last line adds impact or a new idea.

A Limerick

There was an Old Man with a beard,
Who said, 'It is just as I feared! –
Two Owls and a Hen,
Four Larks and a Wren
Have all built their nests in my beard!'

Edward Lear

A Cinquain

Moon Shadows

Still as
On windless nights
The moon-cast shadows are,
So still will be my heart when I
Am dead.

Adelaide Crapsey

A Modern Haiku

Christmas

Glass balls and glowing lights.
Dead tree in living room.
Killed to honour birth.

Ron Loeffler

Reading Poetry

A **tanka** is similar to a haiku. It usually describes a special part of an everyday moment or event. For example, a rainbow, or a leaf falling from a tree. The last line gives the poem a twist or surprises the reader.

A **shape poem** uses the layout of the words to reflect the poem's subject.

A **rap** is a modern performance poem with a fast pace. It has a strong rhythm, similar to the rhythm of reggae music. It usually expresses an opinion about its subject. Some examples you could read aloud are *Haircut Rap* by Valerie Bloom and *Gran, Can You Rap?* by Jack Ousbey.

Free verse is a modern form of poem which follows no rules. It can have any rhythm and it may or may not rhyme.

A **monologue** is a poem written as if the poet or the subject is speaking. Pam Ayres is well known for her monologues such as *I Wish I'd Looked After Me Teeth* and *Dolly on the Dustcart*.

Genres

The genre of a poem is its subject matter, theme and purpose. Poems from the same genre can have different forms. For example, elegies and epitaphs have the same genre: remembering someone or something that has gone.

An **elegy** can be about a person, animal, plant, or anything that has died or no longer exists. It praises the subject and mourns it.

Like elegies, **epitaphs** are about a dead person or animal. But, they do not always praise the subject. Some epitaphs are humorous.

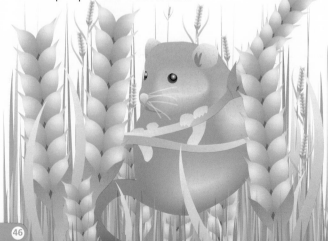

A Shape Poem

The Mouse's Tale

"Fury said to
a mouse, That
he met in the
house, "Let
us both go
to law: I
will prose-
cute *you*. –
Come, I'll
take no den-
ial; We
must have
the trial:
For really
this morn-
ning I've
nothing
to do."
Said the
mouse to
the cur,
'Such a
trial, dear
sir, With
no jury
or judge,
would
be wast-
ing our
breath.'
'I'll be
judge,
I'll be
jury,'
said
cun-
ning
old
Fury:
'I'll
try
the
whole
cause,
and
con-
demn
you to
death."

from *Alice's Adventures in Wonderland*
by Lewis Carroll

Common Themes

The theme of a poem is not the same thing as its subject. A poem may have more than one theme. The theme may be the hidden meaning.

Read the poem below. The subject of this poem is a snail, however, the theme is more general: it is about people being hasty but careless, in contrast to those who take more time and care.

> **Upon the Snail**
>
> She goeth but softly, but she goeth sure;
>   She stumbles not as stronger creatures do:
> Her journey's shorter, so she may endure
>   Better than they which do much further go.
>
> She makes no noise, but stilly seizeth on
>   The flower or herb appointed for her food,
> The which she quietly doth feed upon
>   While others range, and gare*, but find
>   no good.
>
> And though she doth but very softly go,
>   However, 'tis not fast nor slow, but sure;
> And certainly they that do travel so,
>   The prize they do aim at that they do
>   procure.
>
> John Bunyan
>
> *gare – gaze about

The table below lists some common themes of poems, with an example of a poem based on each theme. Other common themes which you should look out for include birth, celebration, childhood, journeys, love and power.

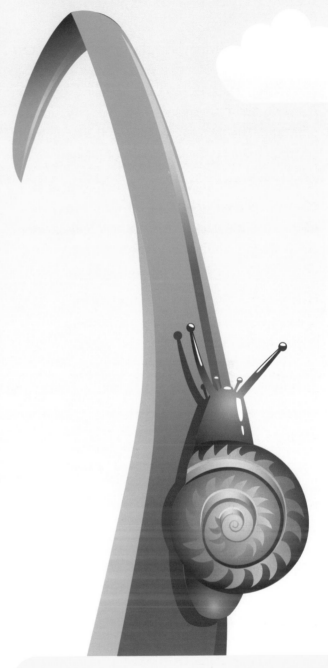

Try to read some of the poems suggested here to help you to understand the themes and subjects of poetry.

Theme	Example of Poem	Subject
Choices and consequences	*The Road Not Taken* by Robert Frost	A fork junction in a road
Growing old	*Past and Present* by Thomas Hood	Memories
Nature	*Daffodils* by William Wordsworth	Daffodils
Rest / leisure	*Leisure* by W. H. Davies	The sights we miss if we're always hurrying
War being pointless	*Futility* by Wilfred Owen	A fallen soldier

Reading Poetry

Rhythm

Poems have a rhythm. The rhythm of a poem can create the impression of a kind of movement, such as dancing, galloping, rocking, swinging, or a train travelling. Or, it can create a feeling of peacefulness and calm. The rhythm can change throughout the poem to create different moods or images.

In *The Wind in the Willows*, Kenneth Grahame gives the poem *Ducks' Ditty* a rhythm which sounds like the ducks paddling their feet as they swim around, and bobbing their tails up and down as they look for food under the water:

> Ducks' tails, drakes' tails,
> Yellow feet a-quiver,
> Yellow bills all out of sight
> Busy in the river!

 Reading a poem aloud will help you to notice its rhythm.

How Poets Create Rhythm

Rhythm is created in a poem through…
- the lengths of the lines – very long lines tend to create a slow rhythm, and very short lines tend to create a fast rhythm
- rhyme – the rhyme pattern affects how you read a poem. For example, a regular rhyme which is repeated often can create a walking or marching rhythm
- language features such as alliteration (words beginning with the same sound) and onomatopoeia (words sounding like their meaning – see page 50).

Try reading this poem aloud; it is almost impossible to read it quickly:

Noon

The mid-day hour of twelve the clock counts o'er,
  A sultry stillness lulls the air asleep;
The very buzz of flies is heard no more,
  Nor faintest wrinkles o'er the waters creep.
Like one large sheet of glass the waters shine,
  Reflecting on their face the burnt sunbeam:
The very fish their sporting play decline,
  Seeking the willow-shadows 'side the stream.
And, where the hawthorn branches o'er the pool,
  The little bird, forsaking song and nest,
Flutters on dripping twigs his limbs to cool,
  And splashes in the stream his burning breast.
O, free from thunder, for a sudden shower,
  To cherish nature in this noon-day hour!

John Clare (from *The Village Minstrel and Other Poems*)

- The poet uses long lines to create a rhythm which suggests a still, hot, humid summer's day.
- Alternate lines (every other line) rhyme. The rhyming sounds are long vowels.
- Alliteration of words beginning with 's' gives a slow, almost still, rhythm (see page 50).

Pussy said to the Owl, 'You elegant fowl…

48

Reading Poetry

Rhyme

When words rhyme, their final phonemes (see page 17) are the same, although they might be spelled differently, for example…

– cold / gold / rolled / bowled
– church / perch / birch
– I'm / chime / climb
– machine / green / clean

A half rhyme is when words end with sounds which are similar, but not quite the same, for example…

– harm / warm
– dawn / form
– grand / found
– mind / friend

Common Rhyme Patterns

Here are some examples of common rhyme patterns in poems:

Couplets

> Monday's child is fair of face,
> Tuesday's child is full of grace,
> Wednesday's child is full of woe,
> Thursday's child has far to go
>
> from *Monday's Child*, Anonymous

　　Rhyme of the first couplet.
　　Rhyme of the second couplet.

Alternate Lines

> Like as the waves make towards the pebbled shore,
> So do our minutes hasten to their end;
> Each changing place with that which goes before,
> In sequent toil all forwards do contend.
>
> from *Sonnet LX* by William Shakespeare

　　Rhyme of one set of alternate lines.
　　Rhyme of another set of alternate lines.

Internal Rhyme

Internal rhyme is when words in the same line rhyme or half-rhyme:

> Pussy said to the Owl, 'You elegant fowl!
> 　How charmingly sweet you sing!
> O let us be married! too long we have tarried
> 　But what shall we do for a ring?'
>
> from *The Owl and the Pussycat* by Edward Lear

　　Rhyme within a line.
　　Rhyme within a line.
　　Rhyme of alternate lines.

Sometimes poets use a mixture of rhyme patterns to create an effect. In the poem above, the use of internal rhyme helps to create humour. When you are reading a poem, look at the rhyme pattern used (if any) and think about its effect.

49

Reading Poetry

Language

The language used in poems creates different effects and feelings.

Poets use figurative language to create an image in the reader's mind. Figurative language includes comparisons (similes), metaphors and kennings.

A **comparison** is when one thing is compared to another using the linking words 'as' or 'like':
– Teeth <u>like</u> splinters.
– <u>Like</u> ships in the night.
– As cold <u>as</u> stone.

A **metaphor** says that one thing is another:
– The snow was a cloak of white.
– The army of ants.
– The room, a rainbow of colour…

Personification is when a writer describes something as if it were human; an object is given human qualities or characteristics. For example…
– The flowers tried to touch the Sun.
– The fog wrapped me in its blanket.

The following poem is about trees. The poet has used personification to give the trees human qualities.

> The Silver Birch is a dainty lady,
> She wears a satin gown…
>
> The English oak is a sturdy fellow,
> He gets his green coat late;
>
> from *A Child's Song in Spring* by Edith Nesbit

Kennings come from Old English and Old Norse poetry. A kenning is a poetic phrase which is used instead of the name of something, for example…

– 'Wave swimmer' to mean ship
– 'World candle' to mean the Sun.

Different kennings could be used to focus on different qualities of an object. Compare the following examples to those above:
– 'Warrior carrier' to mean ship
– 'Life light' to mean the Sun.

 Look out for examples of figurative language when you are reading poems and think about the picture they help you to imagine.

Mood and Atmosphere

Mood and atmosphere in a poem are created through…
• the rhythm
• the rhyme
• the images conjured up by words
• the use of comparisons, metaphors, etc.
• the sounds of words (alliteration, assonance and onomatopoeia – see below).

Alliteration is when the same initial sound is repeated in a string of words. For example…
– The <u>f</u>ragrance of <u>f</u>resh <u>f</u>lowers.
– <u>Sh</u>rieking and <u>sh</u>outing and <u>sh</u>aking uncontrollably.

Alliteration can create rhythm, or a certain tone or feeling. For example, a string of words beginning with a 'k' sound could seem harsh or threatening:
– The <u>c</u>ruel <u>c</u>old <u>c</u>ut through us.

Onomatopoeia is when a word sounds like the thing it describes. For example…
– splash, buzz, roar.

The Tyger

Tyger! Tyger! burning bright
In the forests of the night,
What immortal hand or eye
Could frame thy fearful symmetry?

In what distant deeps or skies
Burnt the fire of thine eyes?
On what wings dare he aspire?
What the hand dare seize the fire?

And what shoulder, and what art,
Could twist the sinews of thy heart?
And when thy heart began to beat,
What dread hand? And what dread feet?

What the hammer? what the chain?
In what furnace was thy brain?
What the anvil? what dread grasp
Dare its deadly terrors clasp?

When the stars threw down their spears,
And water'd heaven with their tears,
Did he smile his work to see?
Did he who made the Lamb make thee?

Tyger! Tyger! burning bright
In the forests of the night,
What immortal hand or eye
Dare frame thy fearful symmetry?

William Blake

Assonance is when the vowel sounds within the words produce the same sound. For example…
– C<u>a</u>t in the b<u>a</u>g.
– P<u>u</u>ll and p<u>u</u>sh.

In the poem, *Noon* (page 48), John Clare creates the hot, humid, sultry atmosphere around a pond at noon on a summer's day through the gentle rhythm, and the rhyme of long vowel sounds.

In the poem, *The Tyger*, (above), William Blake communicates the strength and power of the tiger and creates an air of mystery and fear. This is highlighted by the contrast of the gentle lamb in line 20.

Alliteration and onomatopoeia are used to help create mood and atmosphere in this poem:

These words suggest strength. The 's' sounds are harsh.

These words suggest fear.

In these lines, you can almost feel and hear the throb of the tiger's heartbeat. This gives a vibrant living image.

Reading Poetry

Feelings and Attitudes

Think about poems which have made you feel happy, or made you laugh. Think about others which made you sad or even made you cry, and others which made you feel excited, angry or afraid. What was it that made you feel that way?

- Listen to the rhythm of the poem when you read it. Think about the words – are they soft, gentle, powerful, harsh, evil or scary?
- Listen to the sounds of the words. Does the poet use rhyme, alliteration or onomatopoeia to emphasise softness, harshness, power, etc.?

Read the poem alongside. The subject of the poem is a sad one – a rabbit is caught in a snare (trap) and is crying out with pain.

The poet makes us hear the rabbit's cries by repeating them throughout the poem. We can picture the animal's distress by descriptions such as 'his paw is in the snare' and 'wrinkling up his little face'.

The words 'crying', 'afraid' and 'little face' make us feel sympathy for the rabbit. The exclamations (e.g. 'Little One!') communicate the poet's desperation and frustration at not being able to find the rabbit.

The Snare

I hear a sudden cry of pain!
There is a rabbit in a snare:
Now I hear the cry again,
But I cannot tell from where.

But I cannot tell from where
He is calling out for aid!
Crying on the frightened air,
Making everything afraid!

Making everything afraid!
Wrinkling up his little face!
And he cries again for aid;
– and I cannot find the place!

And I cannot find the place
Where his paw is in the snare!
Little One! Oh, Little One!
I am searching everywhere!

from Songs from the Clay by James Stephens

Points of View

Some poems communicate a message, idea or point of view. This is often a political point, such as being against war, or the importance of freedom and equality. Some poems communicate messages directly; others have layers of meaning.

On the surface, a poem may seem to be about something quite simple, such as a dull, rainy day. However, it might have another, deeper meaning, perhaps using the rainy day as a metaphor for something else (e.g. a person who is depressed or lonely).

Humorous Verse

Poems can produce humour in different ways. A poem may include…

- a **funny situation** – a short story about something amusing that took place
- a **funny comment** on an ordinary situation – words and imagery can make an everyday situation amusing
- **play on words** – words can suggest other meanings, e.g. the poem *A Trip to Morrow*, could be about a trip to a place called Morrow, or a trip taken the next day (tomorrow)
- a **tongue twister** – a silly poem or rhyme that uses very similar words or alliteration, which make it difficult to read aloud
- **nonsense verse** – a poem which has no real meaning. This can be far-fetched and silly and often appears in the form of a limerick.

Here are some examples of humorous verse:

The Ptarmigan

The Ptarmigan is strange –
As strange as strange can be;
Never sits on ptelephone poles
Or roosts upon a ptree.
And the way he ptakes pto spelling
Is the strangest thing pto me.

Anonymous

This poem makes a funny comment on the peculiar spelling of a bird's name. The silent 'p' in 'ptarmigan' is used in all the words beginning with 't', which makes it humorous.

The Greengrocer's Love Song

Do you carrot all for me?
My heart beets for you.
With your turnip nose
And your radish face
You are a peach.
If we cantaloupe
Lettuce marry.
Weed make a swell pear.

Anonymous

The names of fruits and vegetables are used in an amusing way in this poem instead of the words that should be used (play on words). They are used cleverly so that when we read the poem, we can easily tell which words have been replaced.

Peter Piper

Peter Piper picked a peck of pickled peppers.
A peck of pickled peppers Peter Piper picked.
If Peter Piper picked a peck of pickled peppers,
where's the peck of pickled peppers Peter Piper picked?

Anonymous

This tongue-twister is very difficult to say aloud.

A Sea-serpent Saw a Big Tanker

A sea-serpent saw a big tanker,
Bit a hole in her side and then sank her.
    It swallowed the crew
    In a minute or two,
And then picked its teeth with the anchor.

Anonymous

This limerick is funny because it uses rhyme to bring in funny ideas. The final line emphasises the humour.

Reading Poetry

Responding

When you are asked to respond to a poem which you have read, you should think about the following:

- Poetic form.
- Subject and theme.
- Hidden messages or opinions.
- Language and why it has been used.
- Effects created by the sounds of words. (alliteration etc.) and figurative language.
- Mood or atmosphere.
- Rhythm and rhyme.
- Humour.
- How the poem makes you feel.

You may be asked to write a **commentary** on the poem. This means that you should describe the theme and subject and what happens in the poem. Describe any layers of meaning which you notice, effects such as mood, atmosphere and feelings and say how the poet creates them. You should refer to certain parts of the poem, and use quotes to back up the points you make. You could talk about any of the points listed above.

Read the poem carefully before you try to respond to it. You will be asked to back up your answers with evidence from the poem. For example, if you are asked what message the poem is trying to convey, you should give your answer and a reason for your answer which comes from the text.

Example

> ### Tractor in Grandeur
>
> Great tracked tyres trundling – treading
> Its engine throbbing,
> Hauling the trailer, piled high –
> Leaving a trail of cow dung.

1 What do you think this poem is about? Tick the correct box.
- **a)** A tractor being fixed. ☐
- **b)** A tractor pulling a trailer along. ☑
- **c)** A tractor in a barn. ☐

2 Choose one phrase from the poem which tells you this.
'Hauling the trailer.'

3 Give an example of alliteration from the poem.
Tracked tyres trundling – treading.

Structure of Stories

At the beginning of a story the reader needs to know about...
- the main character
- the setting
- the background of the story (some – but not all – of the events which have already happened; some of these can be revealed later).

As the story progresses, you need to tell the reader more about these things and introduce and develop...
- the personal qualities and feelings of the main character
- other characters – their personalities and feelings
- problems or issues facing the main character and other characters, and how they respond to them
- relationships between the characters
- changes of scene
- the main plot
- other plots (sub-plots).

At the end of the story, you should...
- link the main plot with any sub-plots
- resolve the issues, or resolve part of them leaving something for the reader to figure out.

The table below shows how J. K. Rowling develops the story *Harry Potter and the Philosopher's Stone* in the first two chapters. If you know the story, you could continue the table for each chapter to work out the structure of the whole book.

 This is an example of how a story is structured well so that the characters and the plot are developed as the story progresses.

Chapter	Characters	Setting	Background and Plot	Issues and Events
1	Introduces... • Harry Potter • Mr and Mrs Dursley • Dudley • Albus Dumbledore • Professor McGonagall • Hagrid. Voldemort is also mentioned.	A street in a city suburb.	There is something special about Harry Potter. Voldemort tried to kill Harry. He failed, but killed his parents. Dumbledore arranged for baby Harry to be brought to the Dursleys' house.	Mysterious events. Mysterious people. People do magic. Animals behave strangely.
2	Characters are developed: • the nastiness of Dudley and his friend Piers • the cruelty of Mr and Mrs Dursley towards Harry • the spitefulness of the spoilt Dudley.	A street in a city suburb. The zoo.	Tells the reader about the time which has passed since Chapter 1: Harry has lived with the Dursleys for nearly ten years. Gives more information about the strange events that happen around Harry.	The cruel treatment of Harry by the Dursleys. Strange things happen around Harry: the mysterious people mentioned in the first chapter appear and disappear by magic.

Writing Fiction

**Alice's Adventures
in Wonderland**

by Lewis Carroll

Chapters

Most novels (long stories) are split into chapters.
A new chapter in a story can…

- set the scene
- introduce a character
- mark the end of a section of the story
- begin another section of the story
- show the passage of time – hours, days, or even months or years
- introduce an important event or a problem to be solved
- reveal how a problem was solved
- summarise or end your story.

You can number your chapters or give them headings, or both. Headings tell the reader what each chapter is about and help them to follow the story.

Each chapter of the book *Alice's Adventures in Wonderland* (above) is a different section of the story. The chapters are linked by the main character (Alice) and other characters such as the White Rabbit, the Cheshire Cat and the Queen.

Paragraphs

Stories should be arranged in paragraphs. A new paragraph in a story can…

- introduce a character
- move on to a new idea
- move from the description of a scene to the actions of the characters (or vice versa)
- move from one character to another
- introduce speech or show a change of speaker.

Use connecting words and phrases (like those listed on page 13) to introduce a new paragraph and link it to others.

 You should always split a story into paragraphs. Begin a new paragraph when you move on to a new idea, event or character. Leave a line or indent your writing to show when you are starting a new paragraph.

Characters

The Main Character

The main character in a book is the most important character. You might choose to have more than one main character.

You should introduce the main character(s) at the beginning of the story, like the way in which the character Mary Lennox is introduced in this story:

> When Mary Lennox was sent to Misselthwaite Manor to live with her uncle everybody said she was the most disagreeable-looking child ever seen. It was true, too. She had a little thin face and a little thin body, thin light hair and a sour expression.
>
> from *The Secret Garden* by Frances Hodgson Burnett

Additional Characters

A story will also contain other characters who affect the story in different ways. For example, you could create other characters to…

- help the story along
- tell the reader about the main character
- add interest or excitement to the story
- add humour
- create a contrast to the main character, (e.g. to exaggerate characteristics of the main character).

In *Cinderella*, the fairy godmother is an additional character. She helps Cinderella to escape from the drudgery of her life, and from her ugly, bossy step-sisters. The fairy godmother adds interest and excitement, and is essential to the story.

The ugly, bossy step-sisters are other additional characters who contrast with Cinderella and make her beauty and pleasant nature stand out.

In *The Wind in the Willows*, the character Ratty helps to introduce one of the main characters, Toad: 'Toad is rather rich, you know, and this is really one of the nicest houses in these parts, though we never admit as much to Toad.'

Creating a Character

When you create a character in a story, you have a picture of him / her / it in your mind and you know what his / her / its personality is like. A character may have the personality traits and / or looks of people you know, or you could make them up. You need to communicate your character's nature and appearance to the reader.

There are different ways of telling the reader about a character, for example…

- through you (the author) as the narrator:
  - Once upon a time, there was a little girl called Jessie, whose pretty face and sweet nature were rare qualities in the village of Bogdonstone.
- through the main character as the narrator:
  - I, Henry Ginger, was only 12 when it happened – a young, naïve boy with little – or no – confidence.
- through another character's speech:
  - 'You're a smart young woman, Helena', William said firmly, then sighed as if he had given up. 'You should have worked this out.'

Writing Fiction

You can give the character a name which helps to portray the character's personality. Here are some examples from real books:

Character's Name	What the Name Suggests
Malfoy (the *Harry Potter* series by J. K. Rowling)	An unpleasant character: 'Mal' comes from French, meaning 'bad'.
Cruella de Vil (*The 101 Dalmatians* by Dodie Smith)	A cruel character: the first name includes 'cruel' and the two parts to the surname form 'devil'.
Scrooge (*A Christmas Carol* by Charles Dickens)	A mean character: sounds mean and tight-fisted.

To describe a character's appearance and personality, you can…
- use adjectives – describing words, e.g. small, beautiful, funny, miserable
- use comparisons – compare the character to someone / something, e.g. 'he stood out like a sore thumb'
- use metaphors – say that someone is something else, e.g. 'he was the apple of her eye'
- write about the character's actions and thoughts
- show how others respond to the character and how he or she responds to the other characters.

Read this passage. It shows how the main character's appearance and personality are communicated to the reader.

Oh! But he was a tight-fisted hand at the grind-stone, Scrooge! a squeezing, wrenching, grasping, scraping, clutching, covetous old sinner! Hard and sharp as flint, from which no steel had ever struck out generous fire; secret, and self-contained, and solitary as an oyster. The cold within him froze his old features, nipped his pointed nose, shrivelled his cheek, stiffened his gait; made his eyes red, his thin lips blue; and spoke out shrewdly in his grating voice.

Nobody ever stopped him in the street to say, with gladsome looks, 'My dear Scrooge, how are you? When will you come to see me?' No beggars implored him to bestow a trifle, no children asked him what it was o'clock, no man or woman ever once in all his life inquired the way to such and such a place, of Scrooge.

from *A Christmas Carol* by Charles Dickens

____ Metaphor

____ Adjectives

____ Similes

____ Comparison of character with cold and ice

____ How other people respond to the character

Setting the Scene

The setting of a story includes…
- the place where the story takes place
- the time in which the story takes place.

The narrator or a character can give information about the setting. Read the passage below:

> It must have been a hundred years ago, in the city of London, that it happened. It all began in one little house – one in a row of many – huddled within the dark, dirty streets of London. In this house lived a little boy named Michael Lawrence, a well-mannered boy who, despite his run-down home, his ragged clothes and his poor family, lived very happily.

This short passage tells us that…
- the setting is in London
- the main character lives in a small terraced house
- the setting is at the beginning of the 20th century.

You can use dialogue (conversation) to tell the reader about the setting, as in the following passage:

'Yes,' said Tom bluntly, on opening the front door. 'What d'you want?'

A harassed middle-aged woman in a green coat and felt hat stood on his step. He glanced at the armband on her sleeve. She gave him an awkward smile.

'I'm the Billeting Officer for this area,' she began.

'Oh yes, and what's that got to do wi' me?'

She flushed slightly, 'Well, Mr, Mr…'

'Oakley. Thomas Oakley.'

'Ah, thank you, Mr Oakley.' She paused and took a deep breath. 'Mr Oakley, with the declaration of war imminent …'

Tom waved his hand. 'I knows all that. Git to the point. What d'you want?' He noticed a small boy at her side.

'It's him I've come about,' she said. 'I'm on my way to your village hall with the others.'

'What others?'

She stepped to one side. Behind the large iron gate which stood at the end of the graveyard was a small group of children.

from Goodnight Mister Tom by Michelle Magorian

This passage does not say immediately where or when the story is set. But, from the following clues, we can work out that the time is just before the Second World War:
- 'I'm the Billeting Officer for this area,'
- '…the declaration of war imminent…'

There is also some information about the place. Tom Oakley lives in a house near a graveyard. During the Second World War, children from cities were sent to the country where it was safer. The woman mentions the village hall, so we know the setting is a country village.

 You can use narrative and dialogue to communicate the setting of a story, to link the setting to the characters and to introduce the plot.

Writing Fiction

The Passage of Time

Stories can take place over a period of days, months or years. Sometimes a story can take place over just a few hours.

One way in which you can show how time passes is to begin a paragraph or chapter with a 'time' phrase. This can act as a connective with the previous chapter or paragraph. For example…

- – As soon as the meal was over…
- – That afternoon…
- – On the way back…
- – A week passed…
- – It seemed like hours later…
- – After six months…
- – Next day…
- – Nearly ten years had passed…

Flashbacks

You might want to use **flashbacks** in your story. A flashback can be about something which took place before the story began, or it can flash back to a time earlier on in the story, in an earlier chapter.

A flashback may be…

- a dream
- a letter
- a news report
- someone talking about his or her memories of the past.

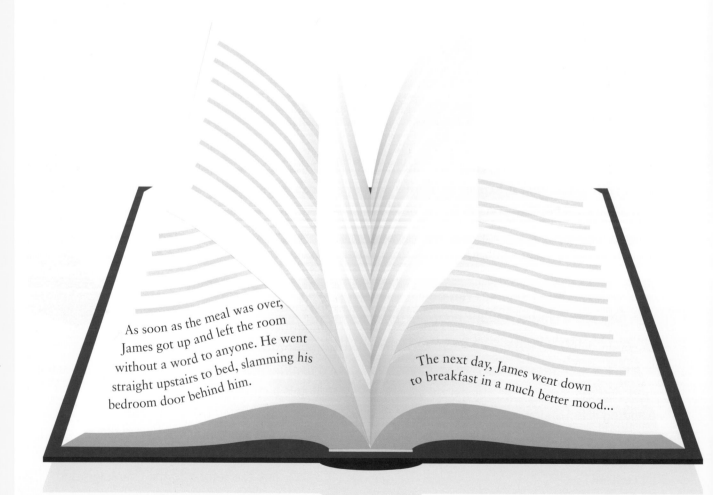

As soon as the meal was over, James got up and left the room without a word to anyone. He went straight upstairs to bed, slamming his bedroom door behind him.

The next day, James went down to breakfast in a much better mood…

Writing Fiction

Opening a Story

The opening of a story is very important. It should catch the readers' interest and make them want to read on. The opening prepares the readers for the story which develops. You could use description which connects characters with the setting and introduces ideas and events, as in this passage:

> The village of Moonfleet lies half a mile from the sea on the right or west bank of the Fleet stream. This rivulet, which is so narrow as it passes the houses that I have known a good jumper clear it without a pole, broadens out into salt marshes below the village... When I was a child I thought that this place was called Moonfleet, because on a still night, whether in summer, or in winter frosts, the moon shone very brightly on the lagoon; but learned afterwards that 'twas but short for 'Mohune-fleet', from the Mohunes, a great family who were once lords of all these parts.
>
> My name is John Trenchard, and I was fifteen years of age when this story begins.
>
> from *Moonfleet* by J. Meade Falkner

You could use dialogue (speech) to open your story, or you could use an event, such as some kind of disaster, celebration or funny situation, as in this passage:

> **Chapter 1: The River Bank**
>
> The Mole had been working very hard all the morning, spring-cleaning his little home. First with brooms, then with dusters; then on ladders and steps and chairs, with a brush and a pail of whitewash; till he had dust in his throat and eyes, and splashes of whitewash all over his black fur, and an aching back and weary arms. Spring was moving in the air above and in the earth below and around him, penetrating even his dark and lowly little house with its spirit of divine discontent and longing. It was small wonder, then, that he suddenly flung down his brush on the floor, said 'Bother!' and 'O blow!' and also 'Hang spring-cleaning!' and bolted out of the house without even waiting to put on his coat.
>
> from *The Wind in the Willows* by Kenneth Grahame

Opening	Tells us...
Explains the title of the book:	Moonfleet is a village on a river near the sea.
Describes the setting:	A small village on a coast with salt marshes
Links characters to the setting and catches the reader's interest in them:	Moonfleet and the Mohune family
Introduces the main character:	John Trenchard, aged 15
Creates an atmosphere:	Descriptions of the village in summer, winter and in moonlight create mystery.

Opening	Tells us...
Introduces the setting:	The chapter heading tells us that this is a river bank.
Introduces one of the main characters:	The Mole. He wears clothes and looks after his home in the way humans do, and he can talk. Mole is a hard-working character.
Sets the scene:	Spring makes the Mole want to clean his house and then to go out into the open air.
Creates an atmosphere:	Nature and spring are waking the animals up. The reader wants to read on to find out what the Mole does next.

Writing Fiction

Person and Style

A story using the first person (when referring to the main character) would use 'I', 'me', 'we', 'us', 'our', etc. and would read like this:

> I walked over to Simon and took a deep breath. I had to say something – he could not get away with this. But what could I say?

A story using the third person would use 'he', 'she', 'it', 'they' 'their', etc. and would read like this:

> She walked over to Simon and took a deep breath. She had to say something – he could not get away with this. But what could she say?

Stories can be effective written in the first or the third person. Make sure that if you start in the first person, you use the first person throughout; if you start in the third person, use the third person throughout.

Language for Effect

The success of any story you write depends on the type of language you use. Language can create effects such as humour, excitement, fear, suspense and mystery. It can also help you to communicate your characters' personalities and ages.

The type of language you use can make readers find your story interesting and enjoyable or it could make the story boring and difficult to read.

- Use a variety of sentence structures (see page 14): use simple, compound and complex sentences where appropriate.
- Think about the words you choose. Try to think of a word which communicates what you want to say in the most powerful and effective way.
- Use different connectives to link your sentences and paragraphs (see page 13).
- Use descriptive and figurative language: metaphor, comparison, personification (see pages 32 and 50).

Compare these two short passages:

> Chloe stood motionless, then she smiled. She went back outside. She ran across the field towards the farmhouse. She could see Harry in the driveway, playing with the sheepdogs.
>
> 'Harry!' she said, 'Harry! Quick! You've got to come and see!'
>
> Harry looked up, 'What is it?' he said.

> Chloe stood motionless for a minute, transfixed, then a smile spread slowly across her face. In an instant, she turned and dashed back out into the open air. She raced across the overgrown field back towards the old stone farmhouse, stumbling as she ran. As she approached, she could see Harry in the gravelled driveway, playing happily with the sheepdogs.
>
> 'Harry!' she yelled, 'Harry! Quick! You've got to come and see!'
>
> Harry glanced up, squinting in the midday sunshine, 'What is it?' he called.

In the second version words have been chosen with care. Powerful verbs, adverbs and adjectives are used. The sentences are connected with phrases such as 'As she approached…'. The verbs used instead of 'said' show exactly how the words were spoken: 'yelled', 'called'.

This gives a more vivid picture of the setting, the characters and events than the first passage.

Dialogue (Speech)

Almost all stories contain speech. You will probably want to include some speech in your story. Speech can be either direct or indirect:

Direct speech is the exact words which are spoken.

- The spoken words are surrounded by speech marks (see page 6).
- Words such as 'said' or 'asked' are used before or after the spoken words:
  - The shopkeeper said, 'That will be 25 pence, please.'
  - 'I like your shoes,' said Amy to Nasneen.

Other words for 'said' can show exactly how the person spoke. Try to vary the words to make your story more interesting and to help the reader to understand the characters' personalities and feelings:

- 'What are you doing?' demanded his mother. 'Nothing,' mumbled Jake.
- 'Get away from my house!' the old man growled. 'Sorry, I'm really sorry sir,' whispered Tom.

Indirect speech reports what was said but does not give the exact words that were spoken.

- The tenses of the verbs are usually changed.
- The person might be changed (e.g. from 'I' to 'she').

- Words like, 'which' and 'who' might be added.
- Adverbs of time are changed (e.g. 'today' is changed to 'that day').
- Speech marks are not used:
  - The shopkeeper said that it would cost 25 pence.
  - Amy told Nasneen that she liked her shoes.
  - His mother asked him what he was doing. Jake mumbled that he was not doing anything.
  - The old man yelled at Tom to get away from his house. Tom whispered that he was sorry.

This table shows how direct and indirect speech can be used to say the same thing. You could use both direct and indirect speech for variation.

Direct speech	Indirect speech
'I'd like a glass of water, please,' said Zul.	Zul said that he would like a glass of water.
Ann said to her brothers, 'Can we go to the beach tomorrow?'	Ann asked her brothers if they could go to the beach the next day.
'Can someone help me to move this table?' asked Dad.	Dad asked if someone could help him to move the table.

Can we go to the beach tomorrow?

Writing Fiction

Planning a Longer Story

When you are planning a longer story, it often helps if you split the story into sections. (In a very long story, these sections could become the chapters.) This will also help the reader to follow the story.

You can split your story in different ways:

- **Time** – the events of a morning, a day, a week, a year or longer. The events can be chronological (i.e. in the order in which they happen) or they could move backwards and forwards, using flashbacks, letters or other devices.
- **Setting** – the places could be very small (e.g. a room, a shed, a garden bench) or large (a village, a town, another world).
- **Events** – one particular event, one character's view of an event, or a series of events which are connected to one another.
- **Characters** – introduce a new character or develop a character, perhaps by describing his / her past or presenting him / her through the eyes of another character.
- **Ideas** – as you introduce and begin to explore a new idea, you could begin a new section.

- **Relationships** – a meeting between two or more characters. It might consist mainly of dialogue. This tells the reader more about the characters and their relationships.
- **The plot** – an important piece of information linked to the plot. This could deepen the mystery or help the characters (and the reader) to solve it. It could build suspense or provide clues.

Flow Charts

A flow chart can be very useful for planning your story. If possible, use a large sheet of paper so that you have space to add to the flow chart if you need to.

Write the name of the main character in the centre and, as you think about what happens in the story, write down the main events and where they happen. Draw lines to link your ideas and, along the lines, write notes about how they are linked.

 In the tests, you will have ten minutes to plan your story. You should follow the guide to planning that you are given.

Main event 1

_____

_____

Setting

_____

_____

Main event 2

_____

_____

Setting

_____

_____

How events are linked

Main character

_____

Main event 3

_____

_____

Setting

_____

_____

Main event 4

_____

_____

Setting

_____

_____

Planning and Writing Non-Fiction

You should begin all types of writing by making notes and then planning the structure of your writing (what each paragraph will be about and the order of the paragraphs). Most non-fiction texts should have an introductory paragraph at the start and should end with a summary paragraph.

Audience, Purpose and Context

Before you begin any piece of non-fiction writing, think about the audience, purpose and context of your writing.

Audience means the person or people who will read the text. You need to think about…
- their age
- their reading level
- their knowledge of the subject.

These factors will help you to decide on…
- the style of language (formal or informal)
- the type of vocabulary
- which words need to be explained
- whether to include pictures and diagrams.

Purpose means why you are writing the text. For example…
- to amuse
- to give information
- to persuade readers to do something
- to tell readers how to do something
- to explain something
- to give different opinions on a subject.

The purpose, like the audience, will help you to decide how to write the text.

Context means where and when the text is likely to be read or heard. Ask yourself the following questions:
- Is it meant to be read quickly? (for example, a sign or notice in a station)
- Will it be read from a distance? (for example, a sign in a park or on a bus stop)
- Will the audience want to know what is on each page at a glance? (for example, a newspaper or an information book).

The answers to these questions will affect the way in which you present your text.

Writing Non-Fiction

Writing for Different Purposes

Writing Explanations

If you write an explanation, you are telling the reader how something works or how or why something happens.

Explanations usually contain…

- a question or statement to introduce the topic, for example: 'Why do grey squirrels now outnumber the native reds?'
- paragraphs arranged in a logical order to help the reader to follow the explanation – use a new paragraph for each new idea you introduce
- logical connectives which link one point to another, e.g. because, however, so that, thus
- the present tense.

An explanation can be formal or informal depending on the audience.

Here is an example of a plan for writing an explanation.

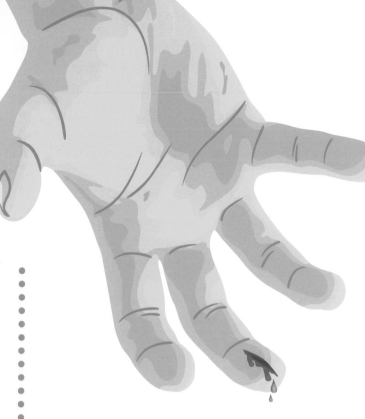

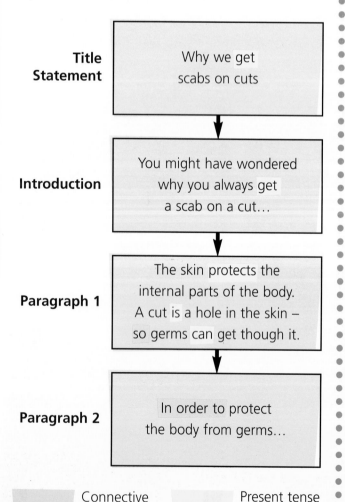

Title Statement	Why we get scabs on cuts
Introduction	You might have wondered why you always get a scab on a cut…
Paragraph 1	The skin protects the internal parts of the body. A cut is a hole in the skin – so germs can get though it.
Paragraph 2	In order to protect the body from germs…

▨ Connective   ▨ Present tense

Writing Instructions

When you write instructions you are telling the reader how to make or do something. Examples of instructions include…

- recipes
- sewing or knitting patterns
- how to play a game
- how to set up and use equipment, such as a video recorder, computer or mobile phone
- how to find a place.

You should begin by saying what the instructions are for. Then list everything needed to carry out the instructions. Follow this by writing exactly what the reader should do, step by step and in the correct order.

- Keep the sentences short, simple and clear.
- Write in the present tense.
- Most sentences should be in the imperative form (commands), for example, 'Fold the paper in half lengthways.'
- Use time connectives, e.g. next, then.

It is often helpful to include labelled diagrams to show the reader what to do and a picture of the finished result.

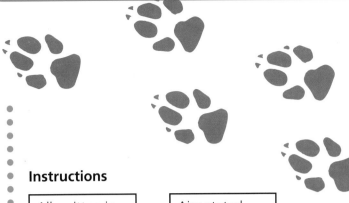

The following texts provide examples of an explanation and a set of instructions.

- [ ] Present tense
- [ ] Time connectives
- [ ] Logical connectives

Explanation

Statement to introduce topic

Why Dogs Chase Postmen

Many postmen have been attacked by a dog. Most of these dogs never attack anyone else. This is because dogs, like the wolves they are descended from, have a strong instinct to guard their territory. So, when the postman arrives, the dog barks. The postman leaves the mail and goes away. This means that the dog thinks it has successfully defended its territory by chasing away the intruder.

Instructions

All written in command form

Aim stated at start

How to Stop Your Dog Chasing the Postman

Introduce your dog to the postman at an early age. Ask the postman or other visitor to stand still when the dog is barking. Ignore the dog until it stops barking – then praise it and perhaps give it a treat (or let the visitor do this).

Keep a weatherproof container near the gate. Leave treats in it and then ask the postman to give them to your dog when he enters your property.

BEWARE OF THE DOG

AL56 WXV

Writing Non-Fiction

Writing Persuasive Texts

Persuasive texts aim to persuade people to do something. For example, you might want to persuade your readers to…

- buy a particular item
- buy from a particular seller
- take particular actions (e.g. in order to recycle rubbish, prevent accidents, care for wildlife)
- give money
- sign a petition
- attend a meeting to support a pressure group
- join an organisation (e.g. a political party or action group)
- go to an event (e.g. a fair, concert or play).

Set out what you want to persuade people to do in the first paragraph. Each following paragraph should make a point which supports this.

- Give only one point of view.
- Give a strong argument for this point of view.

- Provide an opening statement of an opinion through a persuasive headline and opening sentence or a rhetorical question (see below). For example, 'Don't let them turn fields to concrete', 'Would you like to live next to this mess?'.
- Use evidence to support statements.
- Use connectives: because, so, therefore, whereas.
- Write mainly in the present tense, (except when presenting possible outcomes).
- Finish with a summary which might suggest a course of action.

 Rhetorical questions can be effective in persuasive writing. A rhetorical question is a question that does not expect an answer, for example…
– Why pay more?
– Would you want to be treated like this?

Visit the capital for the ultimate weekend break. A city which effortlessly combines history with a truly modern lifestyle, London is a place you can visit time and time again. Visit the art galleries, the museums, or the zoo; admire the exquisite architecture of Buckingham Palace and Westminster Abbey; or enjoy breathtaking views of the cosmopolitan city from the popular London Eye.

Writing Non-Fiction

Discussions

If you are writing a discussion, you should write both sides of an argument. Each view should be supported by evidence. Make sure you…

- give an opening statement saying what the issue is
- provide arguments to support different opinions
- give evidence to support these arguments
- summarise the main points of view
- use the present tense
- write in the third person
- include logical connectives, e.g. because, however, so, therefore
- use impersonal language, for example, 'It is said …', 'It seems …'
- write a summary.

Opposite is a plan for a discussion for and against children having televisions in their bedrooms.

Title (states the issue)

Introduction

Points to support opinion 1

Points to support opinion 2

Summary

Should Children have TVs in their Bedrooms?

According to a survey more than 75% of 5 to 16-year-olds have a television in their bedroom. Some people think this is normal. Others, however, think it can be harmful.

For
- Some good educational programmes.
- Children learn what is going on in the world.
- Children learn new vocabulary.
- Children learn about social issues.
- Good entertainment programmes lead to discussions with other children.
- No arguments about what to watch.

Against
- Children watch TV instead of exercising – could lead to children becoming overweight.
- Parents do not know what children are watching.
- Children watch TV instead of doing homework.
- Adverts for junk food can be a bad influence.
- TV takes the place of reading – reading suffers.
- Children spend less time with family.
- Children talk less, so their language skills suffer.

Summary
Although there are good points for children having their own television, these are outweighed by the arguments against – especially those which suggest that if children watch television too much they do not take part in other activities.

Writing Non-Fiction

Writing Different Texts

Biography

If you are writing a biography, you are writing about someone else's life. You should…

- write in the third person
- write in chronological order (the order in which things happened)
- use the past tense – except where something which still exists is mentioned, or where you want to make a comment.

She had often played 'school' with her brothers and sisters, cousins and friends – but she was always the teacher. She had even seated her dolls, teddy bears and Peter's teddy bears in a circle and set them spelling tests. Peter's teddy always came bottom of the class, while her own favourite doll, Nina, always got full marks.

Autobiography

If you were writing an autobiography, you would be writing about your own life. You would…

- write in the first person
- write in chronological order
- use mainly the past tense
- share your thoughts, ideas and feelings.

I can remember clearly the day Gran took me on her lap and told me gently, first that my father had been hurt, that it was very serious, and then that he was not going to recover. I felt the blood drain from my face. My lips felt cold and numb. All feeling left my fingertips.

Diaries

If you were writing a diary, you would…

- use informal language (see page 40)
- use abbreviations and contractions.

A diary (written only for the person who wrote it) usually mentions events and people not known to other readers. It might also contain words used by the writer and his or her family which other people do not understand.

Dear Diary,

Had a brilliant day. Went to the beach with Dad and Arti. Very hot and sunny. Found millions of crabs, barnacles and cockles in rock pools, and some hermit crabs in whelk shells. Had a picnic – egg and cress sandwiches. We got <u>sand</u> in our <u>sand</u>wiches!

Letters

The style of a letter can be formal or informal. The style you choose will depend on…

- the person (or people or organisation) it is addressed to, i.e. the recipient(s)
- its purpose
- how well you know the recipient(s).

You could write a letter for a number of reasons: to send good wishes, to thank someone, to give news or information, to ask for information or help, to complain, etc.

Formal Letters

When you write a letter to someone you do not know well, or an organisation (such as a bank or other business) it is formal. You should…

- write your address at the top of the page
- write the recipient's address at the top of the page
- write the date in full
- sign it with your full name
- address the recipient by his or her title and surname, e.g. Mr Li, Mrs Patel, Ms Roberts, and sign off 'Yours sincerely' or 'Yours truly'; **or**
- address the recipient Dear Sir or Dear Madam (or Dear Sir / Madam, if you do not know who will be opening it) and sign off 'Yours faithfully'.

Informal Letters

When you write a letter to a friend or someone in your family it is informal. You should…

- sign it with your personal name or perhaps a nickname
- address the recipient by his or her personal name (or Mum, Dad, Grandad, Gran, etc.)
- sign off 'Best wishes', 'Love from', 'Love', 'Cheers' or another informal word or phrase.

12 Acacia Lane
Hatton
HA 6BT

The Manager
Hatton Bank
76 Main Street
HA3 5RB

30th October 2006

Dear Sir / Madam,

I am writing to inform you of my change of address. As of the 25th of November, my address will be as follows:

2 Oaklee Avenue
Hatton
HA7 9RG

If you require any further information, please do not hesitate to contact me.

Yours faithfully,

Anne Clark

Dear Sal,

I'm having a great time here! Great beach and brilliant weather. Our hotel is really cool – it's got a games room and a massive swimming pool. I've met loads of nice people and we've still got 10 more days of swimming and fun!

See you soon,
Love, Annie

Sally James

21 Seal Street

Hatton

HA6 3BM

Threat to Local Library

A petition has been launched to save Oldbridge Library from closure.

Council Cost-Cutting to Blame

The 180-year-old

building was earmarked for closure in a recent council cost-cutting exercise, amid claims that it is under-used and is not cost-effective.

'The money would be better spent on mobile libraries' said a council spokesperson, 'or by providing library services in shops or village halls'.

But villagers say they are strongly opposed to any reduction in library services.

Rural Areas Suffer

'This is another case of the council favouring urban areas at the expense of villages, where the elderly and those without cars are most likely to suffer', said angry pensioner Muriel Reede, 87.

The Council will decide on the fate of the library at its next meeting, scheduled for 22nd October.

- Shocking headline using alliteration
- Sub headings
- Quotes
- Conclusion

Newspaper Reports

When writing a newspaper report, your aim is to attract and keep the reader's attention. You could...

- come up with an interesting, shocking or amusing headline
- use interesting sub-headings which make the reader want to know more
- use a play on words, e.g. 'Parking mad!'
- use alliteration, e.g. 'Disgrace of drink-drive dad'
- include quotations, e.g. from witnesses or experts.

Real newspaper reports often contain an eye-catching photo to help grab the reader's attention.

When reporting the news, journalists have a responsibility to present an accurate recount in order to be fair to their readers. Facts should be checked. However, an accurate report can influence the views of the readers by the way in which you write it (see fact and opinion, page 41).

The tone of the language you use should reflect the subject matter, for example, something amusing or light-hearted can be presented using play on words, but a sad or tragic event should be reported in a serious tone.

Look at the example above.

Recounts

Recounts are about events from the past. This can be the recent past (a few hours or minutes ago) or it can be days, weeks, months or years ago.

You could write a recount to...

- tell a true story
- report news (see newspaper reports)
- report an eye-witness account
- record the main events of an occasion such as a ceremony or a meeting.

When you write a recount you should...

- use the past tense (see page 11)
- tell the reader the order in which events happened
- organise the events according to time, (chronologically)
- use words and phrases connected with time, for example, afterwards, before, firstly, then.

Writing Non-Fiction

Official Documents

The language used in official documents must be unambiguous and clear. It is sometimes called 'official language'. When writing an official document, you should...

- use formal, sometimes technical, vocabulary
- use very few contractions – if any
- use passive verbs where appropriate (see page 12)
- use the third person
- use impersonal language (avoid words such as 'we' and 'you').

For example...
- Private property
- No unauthorised entry
- Trespassers will be prosecuted.

Non-Chronological Reports

A non-chronological report is descriptive and informative writing. It describes what you have observed and found out about a place, an object, a person or a situation. You should...

- use mainly the present tense
- use the third person
- include description (use adjectives and adverbs)
- use examples, evidence or proof if appropriate
- use simple connectives, e.g. and, also, however
- use impersonal language, e.g. 'It is clear that...'.

A report should begin with a paragraph to introduce the topic; this should be followed by paragraphs to introduce each new idea, feature or object and a final summary paragraph. Alongside is an example of a plan for a non-chronological report.

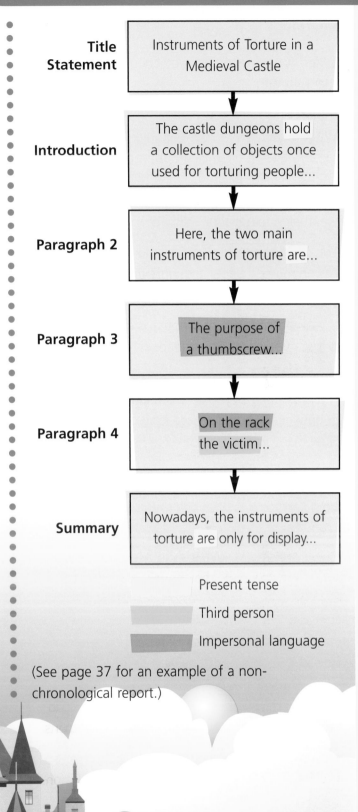

Title Statement	Instruments of Torture in a Medieval Castle
Introduction	The castle dungeons hold a collection of objects once used for torturing people...
Paragraph 2	Here, the two main instruments of torture are...
Paragraph 3	The purpose of a thumbscrew...
Paragraph 4	On the rack the victim...
Summary	Nowadays, the instruments of torture are only for display...

- Present tense
- Third person
- Impersonal language

(See page 37 for an example of a non-chronological report.)

Writing Poetry

Writing a Poem

When you write a poem you should think about the following:

Subject

What is your poem about? It might be about a person, a large or small group of people, an animal, a place or an object; it might be about an event, a story or a situation; it can be about the weather, a material or a situation.

You could also tell a story, communicate an opinion, or communicate your thoughts or feelings.

Tone

Is your poem funny or serious? Is it sad or happy? Is it scary, exciting or mysterious?

Type of Poem: Structure and Length

Is your poem going to be short, long or somewhere in between? Should it have long or short verses? How many lines will each verse have?

It is useful to think about the different types of poem you know (e.g. haiku, cinquain) and to

What should it be about?

decide whether one of these is right for your poem (see pages 45–46). But remember, you do not have to use one of these poetic forms. Poems written by many well-known poets do not belong to any particular form.

Rhythm

The rhythm of your poem should suit its subject and help to create the effect, atmosphere and feelings you want to express. You can create rhythm through…

- the length of words, lines and verses
- the sounds of words: sound effects from onomatopoeia, assonance, rhyme and alliteration.

There are many kinds of rhythm, for example…

- walking, marching, racing, chasing, galloping, dancing, falling like snow, speeding like a train.

Atmosphere and Feelings

What effect do you want your poem to have and what feelings do you want to evoke in readers?

Your poem could be lively and joyful, heavy and serious, thoughtful, exciting, funny and so on.

The rhythm and rhyme patterns of your poem can help to communicate atmosphere and feelings. The words you choose will also help.

Quality of Sound

Some words sound smooth and soft, for example…
- mellow, harmony, glow.

Others sound harsh, for example…
- hatchet, rattle, clash.

You can emphasise the quality of a sound through rhyme, assonance and alliteration (see page 50).

Poetic Devices

Poetic devices include comparison, metaphors and personification (see page 50). You can use these devices to create the effects you want.

Connotations of Words

Think about the impressions created by different words with similar meanings, for example, words meaning 'thin':
- lanky, slender, slim, scrawny, skinny.

What picture does each word conjure up when used to describe someone?.

The writer of the poem alongside has used poetic devices, rhythm and rhyme to create tone and atmosphere.

Alternate rhyme is an easy way to create rhythm in poems.

You can create onomatopoeia and alliteration through careful choice of words.

The tone of your poem will partly depend on its subject. This poem has a serious tone and the atmosphere changes from powerful and quite violent to gentle and peaceful. Each atmosphere is created by the sounds of the words.

There was a roaring in the wind all night;
The rain came heavily and fell in floods;
But now the sun is rising calm and bright;
The birds are singing in the distant woods;
Over his own sweet voice the stock-dove broods;
The Jay makes answer as the Magpie chatters;
And all the air is filled with pleasant noise of waters.

Morning After a Storm from *Resolution and Independence*
by William Wordsworth

Writing a Playscript

Writing a Playscript

Writing a playscript is, in many ways, like writing a story (see pages 55–64). You need to think about…

- plot
- main setting
- scenes within the main setting
- characters
- dialogue.

Dialogue is particularly important in a play.

Useful Words

Act – a main section of a play.

Aside – words spoken by a character for the audience to hear (as if the other characters cannot hear them).

Backdrop – the picture on the back wall of the stage which shows the setting.

Dialogue – what the characters say.

Props – objects needed on stage.

Scene – part of an act which is set all in one place.

Scenery – backdrop and large objects needed to create the effect of the scene.

Stage directions – instructions about what should be on stage and what the actors should do.

You also need to think about the effect you want to create and the emotions you want the audience to feel in different parts of the play: humour, thoughtfulness, sadness, excitement, etc.

In a story you have to create these effects using words and pictures only. In a play you can use actions, scenery, props, costumes, actors' tones of voice and so on, as well as words; these are written as instructions on the playscript. For example…

GRANDAD: (*To JACQUELINE*)
             How are you, my dear?
JACQUELINE: [*Kisses GRANDAD on the cheek*] I'm feeling much better, thanks.

In a play there is no narrative. The story is told through the actions and dialogue of the characters.

When you write a playscript it is important to remember that the audience will not read it; the people who read it will be those who produce the play and act out the roles of the characters.

Planning a Play

When you plan a story, you split it into chapters if it is long. The chapters must be split into paragraphs.

When you plan a play, you should split it into sections called **acts**. Like a chapter in a novel, an act of a play is about a main section of the story. Each act can then be split into **scenes**. Each scene should be set in a certain place and, as in a story, the characters can come and go.

Points to Consider	What You Should Do
Plot	Write an introduction, to tell the actors the background to the story. This will not be spoken on stage.
Characters	Write a list of characters. Say who they are and how they are related to one another, for example, Lee = a boy aged 11; Shana = Lee's sister; Jock = Lee and Shana's dog. At the start of each scene, list the characters who are on stage.
Setting	Say where the story is set and where each scene takes place, for example, *Scene 1: The playground*
Props	Write notes about any items which must be in the scene, including anything that the characters need to wear or carry.
Stage directions	Write instructions about what the characters should do, such as if they should leave the stage at any point and if other characters should come on stage, for example: *Enter Lee, Exit Shana slowly, carrying suitcase.* Also mention any changes of scenery and props.
Dialogue	Write the exact words the characters should say. In brackets and in italics, add notes to explain how the lines should be spoken, for example… Lee: (*Whispering*) Did you hear that? The dialogue can include asides. An aside should be written in brackets and in italics to show that it is not part of the dialogue. Do not include words such as 'said' and 'asked'. Instead, write the character's name in the left margin and, on the main part of the page, just write the words to be spoken.

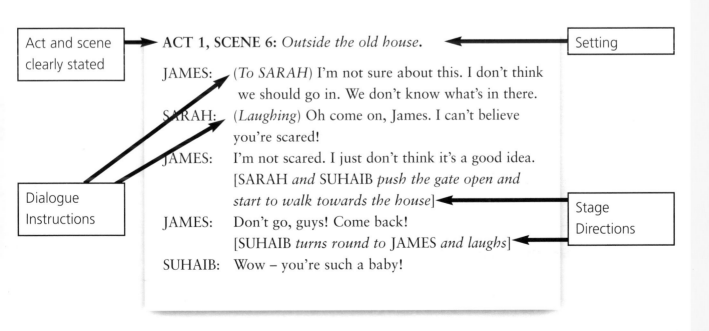

Act and scene clearly stated

ACT 1, SCENE 6: *Outside the old house.*

Setting

JAMES: (*To SARAH*) I'm not sure about this. I don't think we should go in. We don't know what's in there.

SARAH: (*Laughing*) Oh come on, James. I can't believe you're scared!

JAMES: I'm not scared. I just don't think it's a good idea.
[SARAH *and* SUHAIB *push the gate open and start to walk towards the house*]

Dialogue Instructions

JAMES: Don't go, guys! Come back!
[SUHAIB *turns round to* JAMES *and laughs*]

Stage Directions

SUHAIB: Wow – you're such a baby!

Proof-Reading Your Writing

Proof-Reading

Proof-reading means checking a text for mistakes or for parts which can be improved. Read through your work slowly and carefully and imagine how it sounds to somebody else. Proof-reading is very important because it gives you the chance to correct mistakes which may have otherwise lost you marks:

- spelling mistakes
- missing or wrong punctuation
- incorrect grammar
- missing words
- ambiguity
- repetition
- clumsy sentences
- poor choice of words.

Read the passages opposite. The first version has not been proof-read; the second version has been proof-read and corrected. Look at the difference proof-reading can make!

You should always plan your writing, so you should not need to change very much when you proof-read it at the end. You should be checking mainly for spelling and punctuation mistakes.

> If you need to cross out a word or sentence, put a neat line through it. If you need to, rewrite the word or sentence just above it.

All the shells you find on the beach once belonged to molluscs – soft bodied animals with no internal skeltons.

Some mollusks live in the sea but others live on the shaw. There are five main groups of mollusk.

Gastropods have one shell which is usully coiled for example welks and periwinkles. Some coil clockwise and others coil auntie-clockwise.

Bivalves have two shells, for example, mussels and scollups.

Seflapods have shells under their skin for example cuttlefish and squib.

Chitons are sometimes known as coat of mail shells because of there tough oval armer plated shell, which has eight overlapping plates.

The fifth group is tusk shells.

      = Spelling mistakes

      = Punctuation mistakes

All the shells you find on the beach once belonged to molluscs – soft-bodied animals with no internal skeletons.

Some molluscs live in the sea but others live on the shore. There are five main groups of mollusc.

Gastropods have one shell which is usually coiled, for example, whelks and periwinkles. Some coil clockwise; others coil anticlockwise.

Bivalves have two shells, for example, mussels and scallops.

Cephalopods have shells under their skin, for example, cuttlefish and squid.

Chitons are sometimes known as 'coat of mail' shells because of their tough, oval, armour-plated shell, which has eight overlapping plates.

The fifth group is tusk shells.

Acknowledgements

Every effort has been made to contact the holders of copyright material but, if any have been inadvertently overlooked, the Publishers will be pleased to make the necessary arrangements at the first opportunity.

- *Christmas*: Ron Loeffler at 'Haiku for People' www.toyomasu.com/haiku/
- *Goodnight Mister Tom*: (Kestrel, 1981) Copyright © Michelle Magorian, 1981.
- *The War of the Worlds*: reprinted by permission of A. P. Watt Ltd. on behalf of The Literary Executors of the Estate of H. G. Wells.
- *Glozel*: from *Fakers, Forgers and Phoneys* by Magnus Magnusson, reprinted by permission.
- *The Snare* from *Songs from the Clay* by James Stephens, 1915, Macmillan Publishers.

The author and publisher would like to thank everyone who contributed images to this book:

p.12 ©iStockphoto.com / Joshua Blake
p.13 ©iStockphoto.com / Brandon Laufenberg
p.17 ©iStockphoto.com
p.18 ©iStockphoto.com / Steven Dern
p.20 ©iStockphoto.com / Rodrigo Eustachio
p.23 ©iStockphoto.com / Helle Bro Clemmensen
p.26 ©iStockphoto.com / Jolande Gerritsen
p.26 ©iStockphoto.com / Amanda Bodack
p.28 ©iStockphoto.com / Cruz Puga
p.28 ©iStockphoto.com / Miroslaw Pieprzyk
p.28 ©iStockphoto.com / Rob Zeiler
p.28 ©iStockphoto.com / Jason Major
p.29 ©iStockphoto.com / Adam Kmiolek
p.30 ©iStockphoto.com / Kim Bryant
p.31 ©iStockphoto.com / Dennis Cox
p.32 ©iStockphoto.com / Jolande Gerritsen
p.32 ©iStockphoto.com / Jolande Gerritsen
p.32 ©iStockphoto.com / Amanda Bodack
p.33 ©iStockphoto.com / Dennis Cox
p.34 ©iStockphoto.com / Sergey Surkov
p.34 ©iStockphoto.com / Jolande Gerritsen
p.35 ©iStockphoto.com / Will Evans
p.35 ©iStockphoto.com / Joachim Angeltun
p.36 ©iStockphoto.com / Jolande Gerritsen
p.38 ©iStockphoto.com / Justin Welzien

p.39 ©iStockphoto.com
p.42 ©iStockphoto.com / Will Evans
p.44 ©iStockphoto.com / Joshua Blake
p.45 ©iStockphoto.com / Oana Vinatoru
p.47 ©iStockphoto.com / Audrey Botha
p.48 ©iStockphoto.com / Elena Slastnova
p.49 ©iStockphoto.com / Gennadij Kurilin
p.50 ©iStockphoto.com
p.51 ©iStockphoto.com / Alejandro Raymond
p.54 ©iStockphoto.com
p.57 ©iStockphoto.com
p.57 ©iStockphoto.com / Brian Sullivan
p.58 ©iStockphoto.com / Martynas Juchnevicius
p.58 ©iStockphoto.com / Kim Freitas
p.60 ©iStockphoto.com / Simon Oxley
p.63 ©iStockphoto.com / Joshua Blake
p.65 ©iStockphoto.com
p.66 ©iStockphoto.com / David Spieth
p.67 ©iStockphoto.com
p.67 ©iStockphoto.com / Stephen Sweet
p.68 ©iStockphoto.com / Leon Bonaventura
p.68 ©iStockphoto.com / Kim Bryant
p.69 ©iStockphoto.com / Christos Georghiou
p.70 ©iStockphoto.com / Justin Welzien
p.70 ©iStockphoto.com / Helle Bro Clemmensen
p.72 ©iStockphoto.com / Mohamad Saipul Nang
p.72 ©iStockphoto.com / Joshua Blake
p.73 ©iStockphoto.com / Adam Kmiolek & Anna Maniowska
p.74 ©iStockphoto.com / Charity Myers
p.74 ©iStockphoto.com / QW
p.76 ©iStockphoto.com / Kim Freitas

Published by Lonsdale, a division of Huveaux Plc.

Author: Christine Moorcroft
Project Editor: Katie Smith
Cover and concept design: Sarah Duxbury
Designer: Jo Hatfield

Index